Behind
the Eye

Behind the Eye

My Life in Media

GENE JANKOWSKI

Published by Bailey Press, Gulf Stream, FL

ISBNs: 979-8-9987966-3-0(hardcover), 979-8-9987966-4-7(paperback), 979-8-9987966-5-4(ebook)

Edited by Kate Hensler Fogarty
Front cover photo courtesy of CBS
Cover and book design by Molly Mortimer, Mayfly book design

Library of Congress Catalog Number: 2025908787
First Printing: 2025

Dedication

To my mother and father, my teachers at
Public School 69, the Christian Brothers at Saint
Joseph's Collegiate Institute, and the Jesuits of
Canisius University—all of whom helped me live life
intellectually, morally, and spiritually.

When I have fears that I may cease to be
Before my pen has glean'd my teeming brain . . .

—John Keats, *"When I Have Fears That I May Cease to Be,"* published 1848

Contents

Preface

Beginning in the early 1940s, when I was about nine years old, I would walk to the Strand Theatre on Clinton Street in Buffalo, New York, for the Saturday matinee. For eleven cents (thirty-five cents for adults), I could see two movies, a chapter of the adventure serial playing that week, a cartoon, and sometimes a newsreel.

I fell in love with the movies. Westerns with Roy Rogers, Gene Autry, Red Ryder, Lone Ranger, and Hopalong Cassidy, and detective stories with Boston Blackie, Charlie Chan, and the Shadow easily captured my imagination.

Then, in the late 1940s, television came to town! What excited me about the theater—a thick beam of light flashing over my head, carrying stories to the big screen—was now available in people's living rooms. If your neighbor had a TV set, and you wanted your children at your home, not theirs, you had to get a TV set, too. If an appliance store had a television set in the window, crowds would block the sidewalk, eagerly watching this new marvel of communication. That sense of awe cannot be duplicated today, as the innocence of that time is gone.

As I matured into my college years, the excitement of communications stayed with me, and I considered a future in journalism. It is why I eventually became an English major and found positions on the school newspaper and yearbook, which confirmed to me that I had chosen the right career path. But that did not mean my career choice did not have its risks.

After serving as an officer in the Navy and a start in local radio sales, I took a position at CBS Radio in New York City (on a memorable date, as you will see). It was only the second time I had been to the city in my life. By continuing to take risks, saying a confident yes to position after position I was not fully prepared for (despite the blessing of the legendary William S. Paley), and maintaining the moral compass and discipline instilled in me by my mother and father and my Catholic faith, I was able to enjoy a long career in broadcasting, full of rewards beyond measure.

This book tells the story of how a boy born in Buffalo during the Great Depression rose to become president of CBS Broadcasting, the biggest commercial broadcasting company in the world at that time. It touches on the "Mad Men" era of Madison Avenue advertising, the glamor and glitz of Hollywood, and the power and politics of Washington, D.C. Interwoven with this record of events from my career are events from my personal life and stories from the intersection of the two.

In 1978, shortly after I became president of CBS Broadcasting, I received a call from George Stevens Jr., the founder and chief executive of the American Film Institute. When we met in my office, he asked me if I would become a director of the film school. I said yes, and I am still associated with the AFI today. What a dream come true for that little boy at the Strand Theatre in Buffalo.

As I put the finishing touches on this memoir, I am ninety years old, and I am still in love with moving pictures. For much of the twentieth century, there were only three television networks—impossible to believe in today's fragmented communications landscape. We, as an American audience, got our news from the same few sources, as well as our entertainment, sports, and advertising—and we watched them on the same day and time. I was fortunate to meet, work with, and befriend many of the twentieth century's leading politicians, movie and television stars, athletes, newscasters, and newsmakers—and I feel fortunate to share those stories with you here.

Introduction

"**D**o you know what tomorrow is?"

"Tuesday, all day."

"Right. But it is something else. Guess."

"September 11."

"Right again! But that's not why I was asking."

"What do you expect me to say?"

"Tomorrow is the fortieth anniversary of my first day at CBS. I started on September 11, 1961."

Sally and I were on our way to retrieve our minivan from a repair shop in Hyannis, Massachusetts. Three weeks beforehand, we had spent an idyllic August week on the island of Nantucket with our children and grandchildren, after which I had delivered our minivan to the ferry dock. While the van was being positioned for the departure queue, an attendant rammed into it! As a result, it was being repaired on the mainland.

We had decided to take a mini vacation in Newport before picking up the minivan on September 11. We took a guided tour of Rough Point, the mansion owned by heiress, collector, and philanthropist Doris Duke, which recently had been opened to the public. At the conclusion of the tour, the docent requested that the guests meet in the foyer. It was there that we were told that two passenger planes had crashed into the World Trade Center towers in New York City. I commented that the world would never be the same, and that the terrorists had awoken a sleeping giant.

At the repair shop, the manager asked me if I had heard that the Twin Towers had fallen. I could not understand the question! "What do you mean, 'they fell'?" I said. I had a vision of what would possibly be the world's biggest A frame. "They completely collapsed," he said.

Many years before, I had gone up to the roof of one of the World Trade Center towers, where the WCBS-TV antenna was located. It was impossible to imagine that the large tower had collapsed, along with the antenna. Fortunately, there was a backup facility on the Empire State Building, which helped keep WCBS on the air during the 9/11 crisis, although with slightly less coverage.

Not until we saw it later on television did Sally and I fully comprehend the magnitude of the disaster. As we were having lunch and talking about the possible ramifications of what had happened, my cell phone rang. It was our son Peter calling from Los Angeles to check on our safety. He assured us that he had already talked with his three sisters and that everyone was okay. That afternoon, we left Newport and returned to our home in Fairfield, Connecticut. By then, we had also learned of the Pentagon and Pennsylvania airplane crashes. Ever since then, the date September 11 carries with it memories of a far greater magnitude than my first day at the Columbia Broadcasting System!

The year 2001 was also the fortieth anniversary of our marriage, on May 6, 1961, in St. John's Church in Alden, New York, a small village near Buffalo. Sally and I had discussed ideas about how we should celebrate our fiftieth anniversary. One was to write a history of family events that had occurred during the decades of our lives. The genesis of this book, therefore, is from those private conversations. Over the years since, I have been encouraged by friends and other members of my family to write a memoir of my career. In a professional sense, one could argue that my career in broadcasting was an interregnum, as I worked with and for many of the pioneers in radio and television and was still active as new entrepreneurs entered the communications universe. To these ends, I will share some of my thoughts and experiences from my life, risks and rewards both professional and personal.

Beginnings

May 21, 1934, was an unusual and exciting day for the residents of 851 Bailey Avenue in Buffalo, New York! A boy, Eugene Francis Jankowski, was born in a bedroom off the kitchen in the front apartment. The bedroom was about eight feet by seven feet, just large enough to hold a double bed, a sewing machine, and a small chair. Though the house was originally designed and built as a one-family dwelling, as a result of the Great Depression in the 1930s, the house was divided into two apartments, front and back: a door to a middle sitting room was sealed and that room was converted into a bathroom; another parlor became a kitchen; and the front room remained as a parlor. In the unheated upstairs were two more bedrooms. My parents, aunt and uncle, and my maternal grandparents all lived in the home.

I also had a sister, Charlotte, who was seven years older than me. After my sister was born, the doctors told my mother that because of complications, she should not have any more children. When she became pregnant with me, my mother said she wanted to keep the baby, even though the doctors cautioned her against it. After a difficult labor, mother and son survived!

Because of the age difference, Charlotte and I had nothing in common as children. I felt like an only child with two mothers! Charlotte was a built-in family babysitter and a big presence in my early life. If I misbehaved, my parents found out about it. I learned early to behave, or else! In retrospect, I was very fortunate to have a close, loving family of four, since I believe it established a solid foundation for building a future based on strong moral principles. As I grew older and came across various challenges of right and wrong, I seldom had trouble deciding what the proper thing was to do.

As a young boy, I had frequent colds. Eventually a doctor said I should have my tonsils removed, since they seemed to be causing the problem. As it was the Depression and my parents couldn't afford a hospital procedure, it was decided that the operation should take place on our kitchen table. When the big day arrived, I was wrapped in sheets, a mask was placed over my face, and the doctor asked me if I could see the little birdie on the tree branch out the window. Playing along, I closed my eyes and said yes. Then he said, "Try to blow the birdie off the branch." So I huffed and puffed—and in moments I was asleep. The ether had done its job! When I awoke, I was in a bed that had been set up in our living room, and it was there I stayed until I recovered.

There was no central heating, so our apartment was heated by a coal-burning kitchen stove and a coal-burning space heater in the front parlor. When I was old enough to handle the hot ashes, it was my job to empty them and refill the stoves with fresh coal. The original house had a coal bin in a small basement at the rear. However, because of the increased amount of coal required to service the "expanded family," a coal bin was built in the rear of the garage. I used to dread when the coal pile dwindled down to a precious few nuggets. I knew that the coal man would soon be dumping another ton of coal in *front* of the garage, since there was no way for the truck to dump it directly in the bin *inside* the garage. That was my job. It required filling a heavy metal scuttle that I could barely lift, then carrying it over and emptying it into the bin. Not easy work for a twelve-year-old! But the coal kept us warm.

My father, Walter Kasmier Jankowski, did not attend school beyond the third grade. He grew up in Buffalo with a stepmother and stepsisters; he wore the girls' hand-me-down dresses. As a young man, he served in the Army during World War I. After the Armistice of 1918, he moved to Detroit to work for the Ford Motor Company. In the early 1920s, he returned to Buffalo and met my mother, Marie-Theresa Talarczyk. She attended school through the eighth grade, then began to work for her mother's catering service.

Mom and Dad were married on November 11, 1925. What my father lacked in terms of formal schooling, he more than made up for by having an innate sense of curiosity. An avid reader, he taught himself how to construct buildings, repair plumbing, and take apart and rebuild an automobile engine. In a complicated world, he possessed a great deal of common sense. In essence, he was a loving husband and caring father. Nothing is better than that.

Likewise, my mother was a dedicated wife and homemaker who encouraged me to always do my best in everything I did. She instilled in me the personal motto: "If you want to do it, try hard and you can do it!" My parents taught me that nobody owes you anything. Whatever you want, you have to work for it—and eventually, you become the product of your own decisions.

My upbringing gave me a strong sense of self-confidence that I carried throughout my career: I was willing to risk moving to New York City, take on new responsibilities when offered positions I was not fully prepared for, and make decisions that would have life-altering results. Thank you, Mom. Thank you, Dad!

∽

My formal schooling began early. When I was four and a half years old, my mother took me, along with the other neighborhood mothers, to Public School 69 to start kindergarten. She was told I was too young for the morning session and would be placed in the afternoon group with others my age. This was a problem since my mother did not drive. She had arranged for me to go to and from the morning session with a neighbor and four other children.

My mother explained her situation to the school officials and asked if I could start in the morning and eliminate the inconvenient travel problem. What is so different about a morning session and an afternoon session in kindergarten? (Basically, nothing.) And so I was enrolled in the morning kindergarten session at Public School 69, 1725 Clinton Street, Buffalo, New York!

When the school year ended and the class was "promoted" to first grade, the issue of my age was raised again. What to do with me? Make me repeat kindergarten or promote me to first grade? Because I had demonstrated that I seemed to be as competent as my fellow classmates, it was decided that I should be given a chance to see what I could do in first grade. If I could handle the material, I could stay. If not, I would be returned to kindergarten for another year. I stayed and became the youngest student in first grade!

This advantage became an asset when I was graduating from college and entering the Navy. I had turned twenty-one two months before starting Officer Candidate School and was twenty-four when I completed my tour of duty. At an age when many men were just starting their military service, I was able to begin my career.

As far as I was concerned, my younger age did not have any apparent handicaps during my years at Public School 69. My grades were always very good. At the time, the Jesse Ketchum medal was given to outstanding students in the Buffalo public schools in their seventh- and eighth-grade years, as well as to high school seniors. (Now it is only awarded to eighth-grade students.) The medal was established in 1873 by the son-in-law of Jesse Ketchum (1782–1867), a Buffalo entrepreneur and philanthropist who is credited with donating land and buildings to establish the first teacher training center in Buffalo. Ketchum also helped veterans of the Civil War purchase homes and farms and was active in the public schools. The Jesse Ketchum award is the longest running medal for academic excellence in the country. I received the award in both seventh and eighth grade.

I was told years ago that the most valuable piece of real estate I would ever own was the eight inches between my ears. What I did with it, how I treated it and cultivated it would ultimately determine the way I lived my life. If it was fertilized and nurtured by feeding it knowledge through education, I would turn out one way. If I ignored its care, if I didn't feed it good information and let the words of ignorance prevail, its potential would not be optimized. As the saying goes, "A mind is a terrible thing to waste."

My years at Public School 69 were rewarding in many ways. My teachers were experienced and dedicated to seeing that their students were successful with their studies. I believe that a private school education would not have provided any benefits that were not available at P.S. 69. In addition to normal classroom work, boys were required to take two years of hands-on wood and metal working classes, what we referred to as "shop." (The girls took "home economics.") As a result, we learned how to safely use a band saw, circular table saw, a drill press, wood lathe machines, machines to bend metal, and a furnace to melt lead and pour it into sand molds. This was all in addition to how to properly use various hand tools. In the course of two years, I made a crystal radio set, sewing kit, cocktail table, toothpick cup, wall-shelf food tray with inlaid figures, and a metal dustpan with a long handle. Little did I realize then that that experience would provide me with the ability to build furniture and toys for my children years later (and keep all my fingers!).

While I was in eighth grade, I began to consider which high school I would attend after graduation. South Park was my assigned public high school; my sister went there, as would many of my grammar-school classmates. An easy choice, but for some reason I wanted to consider other alternatives. I was interested in Boys Technical High School, which specialized in mechanical instruction regarding automobiles, airplanes, and other engineering-related curricula. One day, my father drove past the school when the school day had just ended and the students were streaming out. He was not happy with what he saw. To him, the boys looked like gang members with unkempt hair and clothing, and unruly behavior! Fair or not, he decided I was *not* going to Technical High School. What next?

My mother discussed my school choice with a cousin of hers whose son, Ben Czaja, was at St. Joseph's Collegiate Institute, an all-boys school run by the Lasallian Christian Brothers. And, as it happened, the school was having an entrance exam within the next month, early on a Saturday morning. As much as I disliked losing my Saturday morning sleep, it was decided I would take the exam.

A week later, I was in class at P.S. 69 and the teacher came to me to inform me that I was wanted in the principal's office. Nothing raised more fear in a young student than a message from the principal: "SEE ME"! I nervously walked down the empty halls, descended two flights of stairs, and slowly entered the office of Thomas Cleary, a big, broad-shouldered man. He welcomed me warmly, then presented a letter to me and asked if I had seen it before; I hadn't. The letter was from St. Joseph's Collegiate Institute and listed the top four performers on the previous week's entrance exam. I was on the list, the only public-school student; the other three had gone to diocesan grammar schools. I was happy. Stunned, but happy! So was Principal Cleary!

Canisius High School, a Jesuit prep school, was having a similar test a week later, and the principal encouraged me to take it. So did my parents. But stubborn me: I wanted to sleep in on Saturday morning, and I did just that. And that is how I wound up attending St. Joseph's Collegiate Institute on Main Street in Buffalo, New York: a decision and an experience that was a turning point in my life!

P.S. 69 was located on the east side of Buffalo, a community composed mainly of second-generation Americans, many of whom spoke Polish or German at home. It was primarily a middle-class, blue-collar area where ethnic prejudices existed, heightened by World War II. At St. Joe's, in contrast, I met students whose fathers were doctors, lawyers, corporate executives, and brewery owners. The classroom was the big equalizer. Grades mattered—not who your parents were. And so, during my four years, I wrote for the school newspaper and yearbook. My senior year, I was editor in chief of the yearbook, played varsity baseball, and made the honor roll! The Christian Brothers also instilled a deep respect for the Catholic religion that I carry with me to this day. And I owe it to my father's distaste from a chance drive-by at Buffalo Tech!

Next: college.

College

After graduating from St. Joe's in 1951, one thing was clear to me: I wanted to go to college. The question was, where? Since we were a "blue-collar," middle-class family, it was fairly certain I would be a commuter student at one of the three local colleges: Buffalo State Teachers College; The University of Buffalo, the largest of the three; or Canisius College, a Jesuit institution with a great academic reputation.

As an all-male, Catholic institution, Canisius seemed the best fit. I decided I would go there as a "Day Hop," or commuter student, and find summer employment to pay for the tuition. Life sometimes is a series of accidental happenings! My choice of Canisius, like my choice of St. Joe's, would have lifelong repercussions of the greatest importance.

In 1951, the average annual tuition at a four-year college in the US was approximately $600. Working a summer job to handle the cost was doable, if one had a good enough income.

During my college years, I had a variety of jobs that helped defray the cost. Not only were the jobs lucrative, but they also were educational. I had to deal with all kinds of people—and all kinds of situations. Over the course of four years, I worked as a landscaper, assisted in home construction, and was a delivery man for a milk company, for which I learned to drive a Divco stand-up truck. I was a beverage delivery man, delivering soft drinks to bars, restaurants, and even a house of ill repute! I was a copy boy for a morning newspaper, the *Courier Express* (for which I had worked years earlier as a paperboy), and a tree trimmer for the City of Buffalo, climbing trees, pruning limbs, and repairing storm damage. I worked in an icehouse where I chopped big blocks of ice, put them in a crusher, and prepared the ice for delivery to restaurants and factories.

During the Christmas holidays I worked as a postman. On my first day on the job, I delivered the mail and returned to the office around noon, expecting a second pouch. There was none! I was told to go home and come back the next day. I soon realized that the Post Office was a very inefficient operation—that paid good wages and had nice retirement benefits. With better leadership, the Post Office could have achieved what Emery Air Freight, FedEx, DHL, and United Parcel Service created successfully. At that time, the USPS was a government monopoly led by political appointees. A good example of government control versus private industry!

The Navy

I graduated from Canisius College in 1955. At that time, the farthest I had traveled from Buffalo was a trip to New York City with an aunt and uncle when I was a teenager. Therefore, the train ride to Newport, Rhode Island, to attend Navy Officer Candidate School was the beginning of a new adventure! After sixteen weeks of intense training, I was commissioned as an Ensign in the U.S. Navy Reserves. Because I volunteered for airborne air controller work, my first assignment was to aviation ground officer school at the Naval Air Training Center in Jacksonville, Florida.

One of the benefits of growing up in Buffalo was, first and foremost, its people. With rare exception, they were cordial, friendly, and helpful. When I was young and in school, racism was not an issue. Everyone played together. Whether on the athletic field or in the classroom, all that mattered was ability, not the color of your skin or the shape of your eyes. After I joined the Navy and lived away from home for the first time, however, I discovered another America! While I was stationed in Jacksonville, I was somewhat excited about being down South and enjoying the warm November weather. I decided on my first free weekend to explore the downtown area of Jacksonville. As

I walked through a small park in town, I saw drinking fountains labeled "colored only" and "whites only."

Wham! What was that all about? It was pure, unadulterated racism. Here I was, a twenty-one-year-old officer in the US Navy, and I was experiencing racism firsthand, for the first time in my life. I saw the same signs on restrooms in the area! How could that exist in a country I was sworn to protect, that declared that "all men are created equal"?

The exposure to racism continued. I played for the Navy basketball team, and we won the district championship. We were invited to Norfolk, Virginia, for the all-Navy finals, and drove there overnight on a bus. My fellow guard on the team was a black enlisted man. When we arrived in Virginia, we stopped for breakfast at a small café and had a hearty meal. (For some it included grits. I learned I don't like grits!)

As I was a fast eater, I was one of the first players back on the bus. Or so I thought: my teammate was already there. I asked, "Did you eat? I didn't see you in the restaurant." "Yes," he said. "I ate in the kitchen." Bam! It was what in Buffalo we would have referred to as a "knuckle sandwich": a hard blow to the mouth. Something was seriously wrong with the country!

At the conclusion of our studies, a black lieutenant who was a pilot was assigned to a naval school in Memphis. When he saw his orders, he told me he was not going to move his family to the South and have them subject to racial harassment as a Naval officer. He went to Washington, DC, to have his orders changed.

My next assignment was sixteen weeks of training at the Combat Information Center (CIC) Officers School at the Glenview Naval Air Facility in Glenview, Illinois. Because I was playing basketball, my orders to go to Glenview were delayed, and I remained in Florida for five more weeks. During that time, I was assigned to be the assistant information and education officer responsible for teaching newly enlisted men naval history. This consisted mainly of showing them episodes of the *Victory at Sea* documentary series, with music composed by Richard Rodgers. I referred to them as "shipping over" pictures, helpful in persuading young men to re-up for more tours in the Navy.

As I was stationed at Glenview from June through August 1956, it coincided with the baseball season! I pitched for the team. On one memorable occasion, we played against the Chicago Police Department team in a charity event to raise money for the families of police officers killed in the line of duty. I pitched one game at Comiskey Park and one at Wrigley Field. And at the conclusion of the series, I received a Ulysse Nardin watch as the outstanding pitcher.

At the end of the CIC program, I was sent to Naval Air Station Glynco in Brunswick, Georgia, for the flight part of the air controller program. The training lasted for five weeks, during which I received orders to join an early warning squadron stationed at Barbers Point Naval Air Station on Oahu, Hawaii. I was stationed there from 1956 through 1958. Our responsibilities consisted mainly of flying barrier patrols between Midway Island and Adak, Alaska, to detect end runs around the Distant Early Warning (DEW) Line around North America.

On two occasions we were called on to search for airplane crash survivors. Wreckage was found of one flight and nothing was found of the other. At another time, we were responsible for vectoring a squadron of fighter planes into refueling transports.

From my years in Hawaii, I recall two terrible accidents regarding the Constellation radar aircraft. In the first instance, the pilot got vertigo when he mistook city lights for stars. As a result, the pilot pulled the huge airplane into a roll that resulted in the plane flying upside down, until the copilot brought the plane under control. The "G" forces generated by the flip tore out the radar dome on top of the aircraft, and once it was free, it tore out the center stabilizer in the tail of the plane. Crew members were tossed around the inside of the fuselage; there were injuries, but no one was killed. After that frightening experience, some of the crew members turned in their flight status and the hazardous duty pay that they earned as a result.

On the second fateful day, the executive officer of our squadron took an aircraft with a full complement of personnel on a training flight. The objective was to introduce an experienced pilot to the intricacies of the W-2 aircraft. The radar crew would also use the flight as a training exercise. The instructor was in the cockpit, practicing engine emergency procedures on the four-propellered airplane. He flipped a switch, killing one of the engines. His student, rather than turn the switch back on, in error, turned off a second engine. Both engines were on the same side of the plane, causing the plane to dip to the side and lose altitude. Unfortunately, the plane was flying too low and a wing tip caught the ocean, causing the big plane to cartwheel across the water, with waves as high as fourteen feet. The aircraft broke apart, spilling twenty-three crew members into the Pacific Ocean. There were nineteen fatalities and only four survivors.

Some of the reports said that more men survived the crash but were attacked by sharks in the water. I had flown home on Christmas leave when I heard the radio report about the accident. There was no detailed report in the Buffalo papers, so I called the Associated Press office for more details. It was a very painful experience, to lose fellow squadron members in such a tragic way.

∾

During one of our flights from Midway Island to Alaska, we began to experience trouble with one of the Constellation's four engines. As a precaution, we landed at the Kodiak, Alaska, Naval Station. Upon further inspection, it was discovered that the engine needed new parts, which had to be flown to Kodiak from our home base at Barbers Point in Oahu. This meant we would have to remain in Kodiak for about five days. With our free time, we decided to go salmon fishing.

It was August and the fish were swimming back to their spawning area. We found a bridge that had a deep-water hole where the salmon were stacked at least a dozen high as they waited for an opportunity to slip into the mainstream and continue toward the spawning place. To say we went fishing would be misleading; all we had to do was cast our lines across the water and begin reeling in the hooks. The barbs snagged the fish, and before long, we had brought in about three dozen sizable salmon.

The question then became, how do we get the fish back to Hawaii without the haul spoiling? We were scheduled for departure the next day, so a plan was devised to put the fish in the naval base freezer overnight. By the next day, the fish were semi-frozen; the challenge was now how to keep them cold for the seven-hour flight in a heated aircraft! We decided to bring the life rafts contained in wing wells on either side of the fuselage inside the airplane, then fill the wing wells with the semi-frozen fish. This was a risky decision for obvious reasons!

One of our crew asked me what would happen if we had an emergency and had to ditch our plane on the way back. I said, "I guess you'll have to grab an armful of fish, hold on, and hope for the best." Fortunately, the flight was flawless, and we arrived safely at the Barbers Point Naval Station. As a result of our adventure, many families had an opportunity to enjoy wild Alaskan salmon, a treat seldom enjoyed in Hawaiian homes.

I played both baseball and basketball for the Barbers Point teams. In baseball, we were part of the Hawaiian Major League, composed of both military and civilian teams. In 1958, the baseball team was going to the all-Navy tournament in Norfolk, Virginia, just as I was leaving for the Alameda Naval Station in California for my release from active duty and return to civilian status. I regretted missing the tournament, but I was happy to be going home.

My time in the Navy was a growth experience. As a young officer, I was given major responsibilities over people, materiel, and missions. Learning how to deal with men from different backgrounds would be a great help when I was given management positions later in my civilian career.

Graduate School

U pon my return to civilian life in 1958, I began to give serious thought to my future. One day, I was reading *Time* magazine and saw a review of the television drama series *Playhouse 90*, directed by John Frankenheimer, who was just twenty-seven years old. TV was a relatively new medium, and I realized it might be a way to combine my interest in journalism with the world of technology!

To do that, I knew I had to receive an education in that new field. In the late fifties, there were few schools that had special courses in television, Syracuse University being one of them. It offered a one-year program that led to a master's degree in television arts. I was scheduled to leave active duty in November, so when I applied to Syracuse and was told I had to start in September, I was rejected.

Next, I discovered Michigan State University had a communications program in radio, television, and film, and one could begin in any quarter of the year. So I applied, expecting to begin in January. Then, as luck would have it, the Navy had budget cuts, and many reservists were released months before their obligated time. I was sent home in August! Had I known earlier, I could have made the September class at Syracuse, but since I was already committed to Michigan State, I went to East Lansing for a September start. In retrospect, I believe the MSU program was more well-rounded, since I was required to take other non-television courses as a minor subject. So I took courses in English and international law.

After I concluded my studies at Michigan State in 1959, a friend of mine told me he was going to Detroit to interview for a job with the Fisher Body division of General Motors and asked me to go along. While we were there, I was asked if I wanted to apply for a temporary position with the Fisher Body Craftsman's Guild, a national auto design competition encouraging teenagers to compete for college scholarships by designing and building scale model "dream" cars. Held from the 1930s through the 1960s, the Craftsman's Guild helped identify and educate a whole generation of auto designers. I said yes, and I was hired!

My assignment consisted of putting on assembly programs at high schools, stressing the value of a good education, as well as presenting the opportunity to compete for these scholarships. My territory was schools in the Northeast, from western Pennsylvania through New York state to Vermont, New Hampshire, Massachusetts, Connecticut, Boston, and New York City. I was to finish up in Philadelphia by Christmas.

At the conclusion of the program, I was planning to return to Buffalo to look for permanent employment. I was asked to stay with Fisher Body and help arrange the schedule for the next year's program, but after some thought, I turned down the offer. I felt if I accepted, my dream of making a career in television would not happen and my graduate studies would be for naught. So I returned to Buffalo and began to seek a position in local broadcasting.

It was frustrating, to say the least: rejection after rejection! Chief reason: no experience. One TV station general manager said I should move out of town and start in some smaller market, as had many of their current employees. But I stayed and found a position with a small advertising agency, at which I was paid to solicit new business, write copy, and place ads on local stations.

This job brought me into contact with local media salespeople. One day, a salesman asked me if I had ever considered radio sales. No, I said. I had my sights set on TV production. Upon reflection, I realized I would be paid a higher salary as a commissioned sales rep than I was making at the ad agency.

Eventually, I was hired as a salesman for WBNY in 1960, a low-watt station owned by R. Peter Straus of New York City, where he also owned a station, WMCA. He was a member of the prominent Straus family, who had obtained their wealth from owning and acquiring department stores. During that period, I got married and was settling down to a new life when WBNY was sold to Gordon McClendon, and WBNY became WYSL. Time to take another big risk.

Romance Stories:
His and Hers

His

by Gene Jankowski

C anisius College, like so many colleges following World War II and the beginning of the Korean War, had to adjust to physical demands on an ongoing basis. In 1951, Quonset huts were still used for extra space, because of the influx of students who had their tuition paid for by the GI Bill, and the school continued to look for nooks and crannies where closets or lockers could be squeezed into existing buildings. An important point, as we shall see!

My freshman year at Canisius began in September of 1951, shortly after the start of the Korean conflict. Because I was a college student and a member of the ROTC (Reserve Officers Training Corps), I received a draft deferment until I would possibly earn an officer's commission as a Second Lieutenant in the US Army. At the time, the first two years of ROTC were mandatory; the second two (junior and senior) years of college were voluntary. Draft deferment was certain if one committed to the third year. Otherwise, you took a chance that you could be drafted.

Since I decided I would rather be in the Navy than the Army, I opted not to join the ROTC in my third year of college. Therefore, I was not obligated to go to summer camp between my third and fourth years. It also meant I had to have a summer job, earn some money to pay my tuition, play some baseball, enjoy the warm weather, and take my chances with the Selective Service Administration (the draft board). And so I did.

It was in 1953 during my junior year that, because of the space shortage, Canisius had put steel lockers in the basement corridor of what was reverently referred to as "Old Main," the original and chief facility of the college and home of the iconic Golden Dome. At one end of the corridor was the student lounge; at the other end was the cafeteria. My locker was about midway between these two highly desirable locations. Years later, when I became involved with television program scheduling, I learned that placing a new program between two established shows was referred to as the "hammock position," an attempt to introduce a stranger to old friends. In a manner of speaking, my locker was in a hammock position by being placed between food and relaxation!

Now here was the best part—at least for a twenty-year-old male college student who is well aware of the fact that there are two sexes. In 1953, Canisius was an all-male bastion, about 2,000 strong. But there was one minor exception. A nearby hospital had a nursing program that offered students an opportunity to become full-fledged registered nurses (RNs) after three years. As part of that program, the students were required to take certain academic subjects during their first year of nursing school—and those classes had to be taken at Canisius College!

It does not take much imagination to conjure up what I saw parading down that basement corridor as I arrived and hung my coat in my locker every morning. It was on such a morning in

September of 1953 when I first saw one girl who shone among all the others. In a weekly chorus line of females, she was always the star. And I never knew her name? "Who was that?" I asked. Others, who I am sure asked themselves the same question, remained silent. Then someone said that she might be Sally Ritzenthaler, Bob Miller's cousin. "She might be dating someone," he said. "Oh," I said, aloud. *Ouch!* I said to myself.

Fast-forward six years later to winter 1960 (date uncertain, because in Buffalo constant snowfall from November until March causes months to mush together like a snowbank). After three years in the US Navy, one year of graduate school at Michigan State University, and a six-month position traveling with a General Motors program, I had returned to Buffalo, and to one of the old college haunts I remembered. Much to my surprise, I found some of the same people and the same beer at the hangout that I left years ago. It was as if time had stood still! And it left me with mixed emotions that I feel to this day. It was comforting to find parts of my past still intact. But it was disquieting to find people there who did not seem to show any signs of personal growth. There are those people, as T.S. Eliot said, who measure out their lives "with coffee spoons."

I learned about those who measure out their lives in beer bottles at the bar. Whether specific to Buffalo or not, it was a habit here to leave the empties on the bar as more bottles were drunk. It was not uncommon to see a bar littered with dozens of empty bottles, even as more were being consumed. In the course of what may have been less than thirty minutes, I saw a number of the same guys standing in what seemed to be the same places that I last remembered them from six years earlier. Within those thirty minutes, the most precious part of the conversation had to do with one Sally Ritzenthaler. "Whatever happened to her?" I asked. "Is she married?" "Not as far as I know," someone responded. No more questions asked!

Goodbye hangout, hello telephone book. There it was:

Ritzenthaler, Sally. On Main Street. Well, nothing ventured, nothing gained, I told myself.

(Ring) (Ring)

SR: Hello?

Me: Hi, this is Gene Jankowski, yada, yada, yada . . .

SR: Oh, no, sorry but I have plans, yada, yada, yada.

Somehow, twenty-six-year-old male instincts sense what is defined as "I'm not available" no, versus an, "I'm not available, so get lost wilya" no. I interpreted her response as the former, not the latter, so motivated by the old saying that "faint heart never won fair maiden," I called again. The rest, as they say, dear reader, is history.

Hers
by Sally Jankowski

The phone rang at my apartment. Both my roommates were out and I was just settling in to enjoy a rare evening alone. Here, in this unusual quiet, was a perfect chance to catch up on my class assignments. After three years of nursing school and the resultant RN, and three years of working in a cancer research hospital, and a year of night classes subsidized by my employer, I had enrolled in the University of Buffalo on a federal scholarship to complete credits for a bachelor's degree in nursing. This, at that time, was my focus and my dream.

Putting down my book and picking up the receiver, I answered reluctantly. Little did I know how this call would change my life forever.

"Sally Ritzenthaler?" asked a pleasant male voice. "Do you remember me? Gene Jankowski, from Canisius College?" Coming like it did, out of the blue after so many years, it took me a minute to make the connection. Yes, I did recall a nice-looking guy, a junior, who, with a few of his buddies used to pal around with a few of my nursing school classmates. We girls were nursing "probies," only spending our freshman year taking the required courses with the college guys. But he and I had barely ever spoken to each other.

Gene had left Buffalo, he told me, shortly after graduation to enlist in the Navy. After that four-year commitment, he had spent time at Michigan State University in pursuit of a master's degree in communications. Now, back in town, he had spent an evening with old friends. In the course of conversation, the subject turned to girls. Going through the list of those they had recently seen, I was mentioned in the rundown. And that had sparked this phone call.

Then Gene asked me out for the following weekend. I was still slightly disoriented and unsure. So, with a little white lie, I gave him a polite brush-off and said goodbye.

Now it was difficult to get my mind back on my studies. Images of a tall, dark, brush-cut, athletic-looking guy came looming back from the past. I remembered that Gene had been sports editor of the college newspaper and had a nice, if not flashy, reputation. Had I just made a huge mistake? I'd probably never hear from him again.

Was I ever wrong! Gene wouldn't give up that easily. And later, when he teased me with the saying, "Faint heart never won fair maiden," I learned that he had a romantic as well as a persistent nature. And so it all began! Visits to the planetarium, a trip to the Rochester Lilac Festival—the most innovative dates I had ever experienced. One night, when I was visiting my mom and grandfather in the town of Alden, twenty miles away, Gene was supposed to come and take me out for the evening, but there was a tremendous snowstorm that even stopped all activities in Buffalo. Somehow, he managed to plow his way through the storm to take me to a German oompah restaurant where, as the only diners to brave such inclement weather, we had the seven-piece band all to ourselves. How could I resist such enthusiastic ardor!

Often, Gene drove me home after late classes, and we'd stop on the way to get something to eat. I was living on a tiny stipend, and it was a struggle to eke out the rent, food, and bus fare. Before long, his parents were feeding me also. They welcomed me into their humble home (heated only by a coal-burning stove) and treated me with great kindness. I hadn't felt so nurtured and treasured since I had moved away to my own apartment.

Now I was trying hard to impress. I stuffed my feet into pointy-toed, high-heeled shoes and struggled into my rubber girdle, ignoring the welts it left on my skin. At night, I tossed and turned with my hair in big metal curlers so that I could have the perfect page-boy hairdo. Were things getting serious? They were.

∽

After a year and half of a wonderful courtship, Sally and I were married at that little church in Alden I mentioned earlier. We had a small reception at Luders Log Cabin, then left for our honeymoon in Bermuda, where we stayed at Deepdene Manor. I spent almost every dollar I had on the trip. When we returned home and opened our wedding gifts, the money we received was almost equal to what we had spent going to Bermuda. Some risks are well worth taking!

In the year before our wedding, I played baseball on the Simon Pures, a Buffalo team sponsored by a local brewery. The team was managed by Don Colpoys and had a few former professional players on the roster. By the end of the summer, we had won forty-five games, lost none, were champions of three leagues, and won some barnstorming games in Canada and western New York. As one of the pitchers, I had fifteen wins and no losses.

Little did I realize then that this would be my last year on an organized ball team. In retrospect, it was a memorable way to end my playing days. The next spring I was married, and that September we moved to New York City.

Goodbye Buffalo, goodbye baseball! Hello Big Apple!

New York City, a New Job, And a New Adventure

S ignificant dates are remembered because of the tremendous impact an event on that day had on the world, the country, or the state—the good and the bad. Because of the tragic events that occurred on September 11, 2001, that day has joined the list of dates recorded in US history books, along with December 7, 1941, June 6, 1944, November 22, 1963, April 15, 1865, July 4, 1776, and November 11, 1918.

So, too, dates are remembered because of their significance on individual lives: birthdays, weddings, and graduations are important because they represent turning points in family histories. For me, the date September 11 had a special meaning long before the tragic events of 2001. In 1961, it was the day I began my association with the Columbia Broadcasting System (as it was formally then known; the name of the company was officially changed to CBS years later). It was also the beginning of the decades of our lives spent in the New York City area.

When Sally and I were married, I was working for WBNY radio in Buffalo. When the owner decided to sell the station, we saw this as a need to think about the future. I could stay and hope to work for the new owner; I could use it as a reason to work for another station in Buffalo; or I could move to a bigger station in a larger city. Once Sally and I identified what we believed to be the best position at the best station in Buffalo, we both concluded we could accomplish more than that, and decided to chance a move that could represent greater opportunity.

I brought home a broadcasting manual that listed all companies that owned radio and television stations in the United States. We sat up in the evening and evaluated cities where we might like to live, and which organizations I might like to work for, sending letters to companies in San Francisco, Los Angeles, Detroit, Chicago, Boston, Dallas, Philadelphia, and Atlanta. We also sent letters to dozens of companies in New York: ABC, NBC, Westinghouse, Capital Cities, Ziv TV, and numerous others, many of which no longer exist due to mergers, acquisitions, or bankruptcy.

Because CBS had numerous divisions in radio and television, in addition to sending a letter to the corporate personnel department, I also sent letters to radio network sales, spot radio sales, spot television sales, and television network sales. I received three letters in return. The personnel department said there were no openings. (I still have that letter.) Spot radio sales invited me in for an interview. Radio network sales said to come in if I was in town! The radio station, WBNY, had a trade arrangement with Mohawk Airlines, a regional airline: in exchange for advertising time, WBNY received tickets for business travel. I was given one of those tickets.

It took four hours to fly from Buffalo to New York. The plane made stops in Rochester, Binghamton, and Albany before landing at LaGuardia. Mohawk was not a great airline. (In fact, in the early 1970s, a man hijacked a Mohawk flight from Albany to New York and demanded $200,000—a felonious act. However, someone joked that because it was Mohawk Airlines, the judge only charged him with a misdemeanor!) I had arranged a series of appointments for my one day in New York, with the CBS Radio Network being the first. My timing was good! Management was considering adding a new position to the sales staff, but they were still awaiting approval and asked me to call back later in the day. When I did, they asked me to return the next morning for more interviews.

I spent the night at the Hotel Chesterfield. As I spoke to Sally on the phone, a cockroach walked across the wall of my room. After my phone call, I killed the roach, then called the front desk. They said, "At least you got it!" I said, "It's not the one I killed that bothers me. It's the funeral service his friends are having for him." They moved me to a corner room, where cross ventilation from two open windows made it more comfortable.

At CBS the next morning, I was hired and asked to begin a week later. The annual meeting with network affiliates was taking place soon, and they wanted me to learn something about the network operations by then. My first day: September 11, 1961.

Now the big challenge was to orchestrate the move of an automobile, some furniture, a stove, a refrigerator, and a wife who was expecting a baby to New York City. Which borough: Manhattan, Queens, Staten Island, Bronx, Brooklyn? Or Westchester County? It was a question of affordability, combined with a limited knowledge of the New York area. From a prior visit to Richmond Hill in Queens, I remembered a community of private homes, green trees, and residential streets, not unlike some neighborhoods in Buffalo. But soon I discovered the economic reality of the big city! Rent for a two-bedroom apartment in Buffalo was $75 a month; apartments in New York City cost many times that. That's why I felt I was getting a "bargain" when I found a two-bedroom apartment on the second floor of a private home at 1804 102nd Street in Richmond Hill—for $125 a month!

The houses on the street were about thirty feet wide, many of them attached. If there was space between two houses, it was barely wide enough for two people to walk side by side to a small backyard. The popular '70s television series, *All in the Family*, had an opening sequence that featured a line of row houses that looked just like 102nd Street.

The house we lived in had a narrow sidewalk on each side and was neither "attached" nor "semi-attached," per the real estate ads, as it had a unique feature. When it and the house next door were built, they were occupied by two families who were related. Over time, one of the relatives became very ill and had to be confined to the upstairs bedroom in the front of the house. So that the relatives next door could visit easily, especially in cold weather, without having to go outdoors, an enclosed wooden "bridge" was constructed from the second-floor bedroom of one house to the second-floor bedroom of the other. It was sort of an architectural umbilical cord! Fire codes would not allow such a wooden structure today, and quite probably it was illegal when it was constructed.

In any event, the bridge was there when we rented the upper flat in 1961. The landlord's relatives still lived next door, and by that time this couple was in their early nineties. While the husband was quite mobile and seemed lucid, his wife was confined to a bed that was set up in the living room of their house. There was no air conditioning: the elderly man did not want to spend money on it because he was saving for a "rainy day." Fortunately, the door on their side of the bridge was nailed shut, so the structure became an oversized closet/storage area for us.

Until the mid 1950s, 1804 102nd Street was a single-family home. But when the Korean War ended, the mother, now a widow, remodeled the upstairs to make an apartment for her daughter and her husband, and she lived downstairs. So the apartment was reversed from the standard layout of most homes: the master bedroom was in the front facing the street, and a narrow hallway led past a small second bedroom, a bathroom, the staircase down to the front door, then to a combined kitchen/living room at the rear. As there was an empty lot behind the home, when it was remodeled, they added a small outside upper deck. So we had a little porch about five feet wide that we could enjoy on pleasant days and warm evenings while overlooking a grassy "mini-park."

When we rented the apartment, we didn't realize that it came equipped with a gas stove and refrigerator. So when our shipment arrived from Buffalo, including an electric stove and refrigerator, we had a problem. It was resolved by storing our stove in the basement of the house next door along with the refrigerator from the apartment. When we moved out, we took the stove and replaced the refrigerator with the original one. (The electric stove was later needed in our house in Westport, Connecticut, so we were fortunate that we had had the ability to store it with the "family next door.")

The apartment was up for rent because the young couple now had two sons and wanted their own home. They had purchased a house in Roslyn, New York, and were waiting for the official closing scheduled for mid-September. When I agreed to rent the apartment, it was with the understanding that if our furniture arrived before they moved to the new house, the four of them would move downstairs and stay with the mother. With that agreement, I set travel plans in motion.

Because Sally was pregnant, she was to fly the one hour to NYC, and my mother and father would drive our car down and stay with us. They had never been to New York City, so this was an adventure for them. We then notified the movers to bring the furniture. Everything seemed to be proceeding so well.

Then came the bad news! On the very day I had to pick up Sally at the airport and my parents arrived after a long auto trip from Buffalo, the son-in-law had a serious argument with his mother-in-law and absolutely refused to set foot in her downstairs apartment. My first major crisis in New York City! To complicate matters, my mother was bringing all manner of home-cooked treats, something she really enjoyed doing, and was looking forward to serving in our new apartment. And my father was very uncomfortable in strange or unfamiliar circumstances. I had no idea how Sally would react when I told her the news.

My first thought was to rent hotel rooms for all of us. However, all of our clothes and furniture were in the apartment, and I felt uncomfortable leaving our valuables. Even though I had liked the couple and the mother, they were still strangers whom I had only met a few times. While I was struggling to decide on a course of action, the daughter made a suggestion: she would send the boys downstairs with Grandma, and we could set up our furniture in the master bedroom. So far, so good. What about her and her husband? They would sleep on a hide-a-bed in the living area at the other end of the apartment. Great idea!

Now all I had to do was tell my expectant young wife that we were going to sleep in an apartment with two people she had never met, and tell my mother and father they had to stay in a hotel several blocks away—and, by the way, we'll be eating in restaurants for the next few days. I still wasn't sure what was going to be harder. Telling Sally about the strangers. Telling my mother about the food issue. Telling my father about the hotel.

I gave some thought to how to break the news to Sally.

Me: I have good news and I have bad news. Which do you want first?

Sally: The good news.

Me: Our furniture arrived in the apartment.

Sally: What's the bad news?

Me: We can't use the apartment.

Sally: Why?

Me: We're staying in a hotel.

Sally: Why?

Me: Well, we don't have to. We have a choice.

Sally: What?

Me: We can stay in the apartment . . .

Sally: I'm confused. I thought you said—

Me: . . . *If* we share it with two people you've never met.

Somehow this line of discussion would not lead to a happy ending.

The final solution was not ideal for any of us, but we made the best of it. Since Sally and I agreed that the young couple were not ogres, we stayed in the master bedroom, and they slept in the living room. My parents stayed in a small hotel for a few days, away from the confusion.

And this was the irony of the situation: when I got up in the morning, his wife cooked me breakfast!

Welcome to New York City!

CBS Radio

I n 1961, the CBS Radio Network offices were located at 49 East 52nd Street, around the corner from the main head-quarters of the Columbia Broadcasting System located at 485 Madison Avenue. The radio building contained the broadcast station, WCBS Radio, sales, and administrative offices.

Plans were already underway to consolidate all CBS businesses in a new building under construction at 51 West 52nd Street. The radio network sales offices moved into the new building in 1965, and it was there that I spent the next years of my career at CBS.

After four years as an account executive, I was promoted to eastern sales manager responsible for all sales from Ohio to the East Coast. There were some notable events that occurred while I was in radio. Perhaps the most memorable had to do with Arthur Godfrey.

Godfrey was one of the biggest stars in television and radio during the 1950s and 1960s. In television, he had two prime-time programs: *Arthur Godfrey and His Talent Scouts* on one night and *Arthur Godfrey and His Friends* on a second night. In addition, he did a morning program from Monday through Friday that was simulcast on television and radio for a number of years.

By the time I joined CBS Radio, Godfrey's exposure was down to the five morning radio network broadcasts. He was an outstanding salesman who insisted on doing the commercials for advertisers on his programs. He is credited with increasing the sales of various products from analgesics to cigarettes (He stopped promoting cigarettes after he developed lung cancer.) By the network sales department, he was regarded as an outstanding talent with a standoffish personality.

One day, the general manager of WBEN, the CBS Radio affiliate in Buffalo, Les Arries, called my boss, George Arkedis, vice president of CBS Network Radio, and asked if Godfrey could come to Buffalo and be the guest speaker at a luncheon fundraiser for some local charity.

Godfrey approved the trip. Then my boss thought it would be a good idea if I went along, as the "kid from Buffalo." So I did!

I was told to meet Godfrey at Teterboro Airport where he kept his airplane. We were scheduled to take off and arrive in Buffalo for lunch at noon at the Hotel Statler. Arthur had a two-man crew who arranged all his preflight requirements, so by the time Godfrey arrived, all he had to do was sit in the left-hand seat and go!

For whatever reason, Godfrey was late arriving at the airport, and I knew we would be late for the noon luncheon. Once he arrived at the plane, he took the pilot's seat, the chief pilot became the copilot, and the copilot became the flight attendant!

We arrived at Buffalo International Airport late and were met by Les Arries in a stretch limousine and police escort. Godfrey, Arries, and I sat in the back seat and away we went, sirens blaring, through the streets of Buffalo, through traffic down Main Street, passing gawking shoppers, to the Statler.

While zooming through traffic, my one thought was, *If my friends could see me now!*

When we arrived at the hotel, we were led to a private room where the mayor, Frank Sedita, and the city councilmen were waiting patiently. Mayor Sedita said, "Welcome to Buffalo, Mr. Godfrey." Godfrey said, "Glad to be here, Mr. Mayor. Let's belly up to the bar, boys!" A big laugh and within seconds Godfrey had the town in the palm of his hand.

The luncheon was a sellout. The overflow crowd had to sit at tables set up in the foyer. One woman came up to Godfrey to say hello. It was Aja Zanova, an international ice-skating champion who obviously knew him from a previous time. It was old home week for the two of them!

Rather than leave Buffalo after lunch for a quick return to New York, Arthur was invited to see the latest developments on the Niagara Hydroelectric project. I left that group and told Arthur I would meet him at Buffalo International at 4 p.m.

We left for New York City on time, scheduled to return using instrument flight rules (IFR), which meant we would zigzag, city by city, to Teterboro. Once we were airborne, on our way to Rochester flight control, an air controller came on the radio and asked, "Mike one, care to fly visual direct to Teterboro."

Godfrey said, "Hell yes." The controller said, "Good night, Mr. Godfrey."

"Mike one" was Godfrey's air handle. I asked him how they knew it was him. He said every Christmas he sent grease pencils to the controllers for their radar scopes, "compliments of Arthur Godfrey"!

When I returned to the office the following day, my boss asked how the trip went. "Great!" I said. "And I have an idea. We always talk about 'Arthur Godfrey the talent.' But yesterday I saw 'Arthur Godfrey the salesman'! Why not have a lunch with Godfrey and all our salespeople to talk about salesmanship?"

Another one of my bosses, Ben Lochridge, went to Godfrey and made the request. He responded by saying he had a better idea: he would host everyone at his farm in Virginia, Paeonian Springs.

And so he did!

Godfrey owned 2,500 acres where he kept a menagerie of animals, an indoor riding arena, a horse barn, and his main residence. As I looked over the landscape, I asked how much was his, and he said, "As far as the eye can see."

Godfrey asked if we would like to see a dressage demonstration. He called his stable and asked that his horse, Goldie, be saddled and taken to the riding arena. When we arrived, Godfrey mounted the horse and gave us a fifteen-minute program of dressage. Impressive! When it was over, he gave the reins to the groom, and we returned to his house. It was a great day for all of us!

∾

Frank Gifford

One of the advertisers on the radio network was Millers Falls Tools, a small company in Greenfield, Massachusetts. Their commercials were on a program called *Worldwide Sports* with Chris Schenkel as the anchor. To ensure a fifty-two-week contract, Schenkel and I went to Greenfield for dinner with the client.

Schenkel was great with client relations. Coincidentally, at the same restaurant was another dinner honoring the Boy Scouts. When they learned Chris Schenkel was in the next room, they asked if he would speak to the Scouts. He did. He was outstanding! If he were running for office, he would have been elected. Our client was also impressed, and I looked forward to a long relationship between Schenkel and Millers Falls.

I was stunned when, a few weeks later, Schenkel told me he was leaving CBS for a position at ABC, where he spent the rest of his career.

My immediate problem was who was to replace Schenkel on *Worldwide Sports* to the satisfaction of Millers Falls.

Enter Frank Gifford!

Gifford had just finished his outstanding football career with the New York Giants and was beginning a career in broadcasting. A big question was how he would do as anchor of *Worldwide Sports* and whether he would be acceptable to the Millers Falls people. If not, goodbye fifty-two-week contract!

The best way to determine that was to take Gifford to Greenfield and have lunch with the client. I promised the *Worldwide Sports* producer that Frank would be back in New York for that evening's live broadcast.

On the day of the lunch, I picked up Gifford at his Westchester home and drove the four hours to Greenfield. For most of the trip, he slept in the rear seat of my car. When we arrived at the hotel dining room for the pre-lunch meeting, Frank stood around like a shy teenager and barely spoke. Not good!

It wasn't until we finished lunch and began to talk about football procedures, plans, and probabilities that he opened up and wowed the client with his knowledge and articulation about the game.

Successful meeting! Millers Falls remained a client! Now I had to get Gifford back to New York. To do that I hired a local pilot who flew his own two-seater Piper Cub to Springfield, Massachusetts, where Frank would make the flight to New York. The local pilot was out of Central Casting, complete with leather jacket, white scarf, and big cigar!

It took courage to get into the second seat, and Gifford did it with good humor. He took off and I got in my car for the four-hour trip to my home. I was still on the highway when the program was scheduled to begin. I turned on my radio and calmed down when I heard, "*Worldwide Sports* with Frank Gifford." He had made it!

In 2013, about five decades later, I was having lunch with my wife, Lisa, at the Wauwinet Inn on Nantucket Island. She said, "Don't turn around, but Frank and Kathie Lee Gifford are sitting at the next table."

Not only did I turn around, I got up and went to their table to say hello. Lisa was not aware that I knew Frank and Kathie Lee very well. As we chatted, Frank asked what we were doing for dinner. I said we had reservations at the Galley Restaurant by the water. As it happened, so did they, and he invited us to join them.

That evening the four of us had dinner, accompanied by their daughter and a friend. I noticed that Frank was having some difficulty remembering some facts about his past. It made me think that perhaps Frank had suffered too many concussions during his illustrious football career. After dinner, we had a group photo taken. It was the last time I saw him in person.

In 2015, just two years later, Frank passed away, and the country lost one of its admired athletes and broadcasters. He was one week short of his eighty-fifth birthday. Later that year, the family announced that Frank had chronic traumatic encephalopathy (CTE). To honor Frank's legacy of promoting player safety, they donated his brain to research on the link between football and brain injury. An admirable act to further honor an outstanding individual.

Network Television

I stayed with radio until January 1969. At that time, the CBS Television Network was looking for a new account executive, and the sales vice president asked my supervisor Ben Lochridge if he had anyone he could recommend. He recommended me. I now had an opportunity to gain experience with the leading network sales department. Arthur Godfrey sent me a personal note that said, "January 20, 1969! Nixon is inaugurated as President and Jankowski goes to television! What a helluva world we have in store!"

My time at the network was both educational and exciting. I met some dedicated professional salespeople who cared deeply about CBS. James Rosenfield was my boss. He was respected and admired by his staff and the many clients he dealt with. He was tough, smart, and had a great sense of humor. To this day I consider him to be one of the best network executives I ever met.

While I was a sales executive at the CBS network, management decided to have a department golf tournament to build team spirit. The outing was scheduled for November 11, then referred to as Armistice Day and a national holiday. The tournament was referred to as the "Malibu Run Memorial," after a television series that had aired for just one episode. After that, the series was cancelled! Done!

I didn't play golf, but I was determined to be a part of the activities. So I went to the driving range in Westport, Connecticut, and began whacking balls in order to become a little familiar with the various golf clubs. When the big day came, we gathered at the Stanwich Club in Greenwich, Connecticut. On my way to the first hole, I saw Bud Materne, vice president of sales and my boss. "How do you think you'll do today?"

He said, "I'll probably shoot 105."

I took some small comfort in his response, since I guessed I might shoot 120—if I was lucky. Wisely, the organizers put all the duffers like me in our own foursome, so we would not affect the more serious players. As an added treat, a welcome wagon drove around the course, offering snacks and beverages. This was network golf!

When the game was over, all the players gathered at the clubhouse for the nineteenth hole, and I ran into Bud Materne again. I asked him how he did. He said, "I shot 105."

"Remarkable!" I said. "You said you would do that and you did!"

He said, "Gene, understand one thing. When I reach 105 strokes, I pick up my ball and walk off the course. *Sometimes* I make all eighteen holes!"

That comment put the game in focus for me. Playing golf no longer became a stressful activity for me, but rather a source of fun and camaraderie. Thank you, Bud Materne.

∽

West 52nd Street between Fifth and Sixth Avenues at one time was considered Restaurant Row. A short walk from Fifth was the famous "21" Club, a restaurant at 21 West 52nd Street with a fascinating past and a very active present. During Prohibition, the club was a speakeasy, with a secret wine cellar located in the basement of the building next door.

Next came Toots Shor, a large restaurant named after the owner, Bernard "Toots" Shor. Toots was a friend of everybody: politicians, actors, movie stars, and financiers. He had a large lower level in his restaurant, in anticipation of legalized gambling in New York City. It did not happen during his lifetime.

Next door to the CBS Building, at 41 West 52nd Street, was a small eatery called Rose's. It was owned and operated by a family that understood Madison Avenue advertising habits. It was a popular hangout for ad execs, sales reps, and show businesspeople. Besides the "who's who" of CBS, Gordon MacRae, star of *Carousel* and *Oklahoma,* was a regular, as were actor Dean Jagger and Ed McMahon, Johnny Carson's sidekick on NBC's *The Tonight Show.*

Eventually, Shor's and Rose's were demolished, to the dismay of the three-martini-lunch crowd. Afterward, someone remarked that the CBS Network Sales department was now short two offices!

∞

At this time, I also met David Fuchs, an executive with the news division who wrote presentations for news specials that we had to sell to advertisers. He was great with words, but I had no idea then that years later we would collaborate on a book about network television.

WCBS-TV

W hat I thought would be a long career in network sales ended a year and half later when I was asked to be the general sales manager of WCBS-TV, the CBS-owned and -operated station in New York City. It was another opportunity to learn about local television and another division of CBS. Once at WCBS, I decided to personally visit all the major advertising agencies to meet the people responsible for placing ad dollars on local television. In most cases, they were different people than the ones who placed ads on the networks.

The stories I heard did not make me happy! I was told that some time buyers kept detailed statistics on WCBS so they could look for reasons *not* to buy time on the station. Clearly, there was a lot of work to be done to improve the image of the station's sales performance and agency-station relations. With the help of a new assistant sales manager whom I had hired away from NBC, who was well respected in the industry, we began to change the way we conducted business. We hired better quality salespeople and became more aggressive in pursuing new accounts.

Then one day I was informed that the corporation had hired

the consulting firm McKinsey and Co. to examine the structure of the television stations business. A new position was created: director of sales. The general sales manager and the finance manager would report to the new position. I was passed over and did not get the new job!

Sally shed tears when I told her about the new situation. She felt my disappointment and agreed that maybe I should look for a new position in another company. I called Tom Murphy, president of Capital Cities Broadcasting, and talked to him about opportunities. He said it might be possible for me to go back to Buffalo and run a radio station they owned. Since I had left Buffalo and radio, that had no appeal to me, so I decided to make the best of my new situation and see what developed.

One day I was sitting in my office and the telephone rang. My assistant answered. "Yes sir, he is," I heard her say. "There is a Mr. Perdue who wants to talk to you," she said to me.

I didn't know anyone named Perdue, but I took the call. "Mr. Jankowski, I would like to meet with you today. Can you come to my room at the Hotel Roosevelt? I have some business to discuss."

My immediate reaction was to ask myself if I really wanted to meet a stranger in a hotel room. Then I decided it was a risk worth taking, so I said yes. Later that afternoon, I knocked and entered a small room at the Roosevelt that was not much larger than the double-sized bed it contained. There was only room for one small chair, and sitting in it was Mr. Frank Perdue.

After a brief intro, Perdue told me his story. He was the owner of a very large farm in Maryland, where he raised thousands of chickens. His goal, he said, was to do something that had never been done before: to establish an identity for chickens. In effect, to create a brand for chickens in the same way that most consumer products had brand identities.

What Perdue wanted from me was the name of a medium-sized ad agency that could help him accomplish this goal. I told him I couldn't do that; that we worked with a number of reputable agencies, and I didn't believe that I should recommend one over the others. I directed him to books that provided information on agencies, their size and special areas of expertise. Once he selected an agency, I said WCBS-TV would be very pleased to help deliver his message to our sizable audience.

On the way back to my office from the meeting, I thought about my reaction when I'd first seen Mr. Perdue. Physically, he was slight, with a head of thinning hair, and a beak-like nose that reminded me of—a chicken!

Eventually, Perdue selected the agency Scali, McCabe, Sloves to handle his business. They may have had the same reaction when they decided to feature Frank Perdue in his own commercials with the iconic message: "It takes a tough man to make a tender chicken." The campaign was a huge success. Frank Perdue succeeded in his quest to brand chickens. The commercial was ranked by *Advertising Age* as one of the best campaigns of the year. And WCBS-TV received a good share of the Perdue advertising dollars spent in the New York City area.

∾

When hiring employees, I always looked for people who were smart, personable, eager to succeed, and pleasant to be around. During my time as general sales manager, there was an effort made to hire more minorities. While I was very much in favor of the idea, I resisted any attempt by corporate Human Resources to hire a person simply based on the color of their skin. My career depended on my ability to deliver increased sales each year, so I was determined to hire people of my choosing. Hiring someone to work for you is a tremendous responsibility. Offering someone a job can have a major impact on their life, so it cannot be taken casually. Furthermore, hiring the wrong person can have an impact on a manager's life, if the individual is an ineffective sales representative.

So I decided I would do what Branch Rickey did when he signed Jackie Robinson to the Brooklyn Dodgers. He made sure the man could play baseball first, then considered his race. By setting a high standard, I eventually hired a person who became an outstanding sales representative, not only respected by his customers but also his fellow salespeople. For better or for worse, a sales department and its manager have an unbreakable bond. If the team is good, they push managers up; if the team is bad, they pull him down.

That is why I always felt it was important to look for the brightest and the most personable candidates. I had a woman sales rep who fit the description perfectly. Her name was Gail Trell. She was a Phi Beta Kappa college graduate who had a warm and pleasant personality and a killer instinct. She never wanted to lose a sale. One of the agencies I was going to assign her had a female time buyer who made it clear to me that she did not want a female salesperson to deal with her.

I assigned Gail as sales rep anyway. After the first meeting, the buyer called me to complain. "I thought I told you I did not want a woman calling on me," she said. My response: "I heard you, but I felt you would eventually be very satisfied with her service to you. Give it a chance."

Within a few weeks, there was no way I could make a change. The buyer was ecstatic with her new salesperson. Conclusion: Listen to clients' concerns and be respectful but have the courage of your own convictions. Again, the performance of your sales team is your responsibility, not anyone else's.

∽

Staying at CBS turned out to be the best decision for me. Eventually, the new sales director, John McKay, was promoted to general manager of KMOX-TV, the CBS-owned station in St. Louis. I was promoted and became the director of sales for WCBS-TV and eventually the vice president of sales for the entire Television Stations division. CBS owned stations in New York, Chicago, Los Angeles, Philadelphia, and St. Louis, so I had an opportunity to study the sales procedures of the various managers and gain knowledge about the cities and their advertising communities.

Vice President, Finance, CBS

I had only been vice president of sales for the Television Stations division for about six months when the president of the division, Tom Miller, called me into his office. "Would you like to be the general manager of KMOX-TV in St. Louis, or the vice president of finance for the division?" he asked.

Wow! That was a surprise.

I had always wanted to be the general manager of a television station, so that had a great appeal. "Vice president of finance?" I asked. "How does that happen?"

Miller had been looking for a financial executive for some time and hadn't found anyone he liked. He had expressed his problem to Arthur Taylor, president of the CBS Corporation, and Taylor, who was a history major out of Brown University, suggested he should look for someone he could trust, and think leadership, not finances, for his answer. Taylor had come from International Paper, where someone had made a similar decision about him.

As much as I wanted to run a television station, the thought of moving my family, a wife and now four children, from Connecticut to Missouri gave me hesitation. And on the other hand, being vice president of finance would give a new dimension to my work experience. My formal education was in programming and my business experience was in sales, so a position in finance would give me a well-rounded resume, should I have to seek employment elsewhere. After giving the question serious consideration and the discussion of a possible move to St. Louis with Sally, I opted for the financial position. It was a big risk worth taking, and I would not have to move my family and sell my house. I would learn more about the finances of the station's divisions; and if I failed? Well, failure I felt was not an option!

At that time, the CBS Corporation had seventeen divisions, ranging from broadcasting, publishing, phonograph records, Creative Playthings, and musical instruments, including Steinway pianos, Gemeinhardt flutes, and Gibson guitars. The finance position had a direct line of responsibility to the chief financial officer of the corporation, James Geer. I had a meeting with him and asked him how he saw the stations division and what issues he was concerned about.

Without missing a beat, Geer said, "Your accounts receivables and your film inventory. Get them under control!"

So I examined both areas. As for the film inventory, the stations had contracts with Hollywood studios consisting of thousands of titles with varying contract expiration dates. Some contracts might call for a certain number of air dates over a period of ten years. If the station did not play the films and the contract expired, it would face a write-off, a negative hit to the bottom line! So, with the able effort of some smart computer people, all the movie inventory for all of the stations was put into a database for each station. This enabled the program director and general manager of a station to know which titles he had to air to avoid a write-off.

The TV stations' receivables were about 120 days outstanding, far above a more normal 30 to 60 days. I asked my chief accountant why the days outstanding were so high. He said the ad agencies claimed they were being billed for schedules they hadn't ordered. So they sat on the invoices. Right then, I knew the cause of the problem. As an example, a client might place an order for five commercials to be placed in five specific programs. If the station's traffic department moved a commercial to a different program without notifying the agency, when the bill went out, it would not conform with the original order, so the bill would not be paid. I concluded the receivables issue was not a financial problem; it was a sales management problem. To fix the issue required the attention of each station general manager.

So I asked the division president, when he talked to the GMs of the stations, to ask them what their outstanding receivables were. None of them knew the answers. That got their attention! Then I suggested we not pay salesmen their commissions until we collected the money. That got the attention of the sales teams! They were certain to communicate any schedule changes to the clients.

Within a few months, the division receivables dropped from 120 days to about 60 days. Once a month, all the financial officers of the corporation would have a meeting with the president of the company and give verbal reports on developments in their division. At one such meeting several months later, I put on a presentation where I somewhat facetiously showed that the financial department of the stations division was the third most profitable area of the company, based on the increased cash we received by lowering the receivables.

∽

La Grenouille was a classy French restaurant on 52nd Street. It was close to CBS headquarters and was a convenient place to have a business lunch with a client or colleague. I was meeting with a client there one day when the maître d' said I had a telephone call. It was my office, calling to inform me that Arthur Taylor wanted me in his office at one o'clock. Not knowing what it was about, I excused myself from the lunch, saying I had been summoned to the president's office.

When I arrived, Taylor greeted me warmly, then said he wanted me to become the controller of the CBS Corporation. To say I was surprised was an understatement! I said, "But Arthur, I'm not an accountant." He said, "I know that. You would have accountants working *for* you. I want a communicator. I have seventeen divisions reporting to me, and I need to know what's going on throughout the company."

So I said, "If you want me to do it, I will."

"You may not get back to broadcasting," Taylor said. "Potentially, you might become president of one of the seventeen divisions." I said I was willing to take the responsibility. Done deal! I was now vice president and controller of CBS, Inc.

The next day, commuting in on the train from Connecticut, I sat with my friend John Dolan, who was an executive in the Records Group. I told him about my new position. He roared and said that there would be "a lot of moaning in homes in the CBS family." I was indeed an unorthodox choice for the job! But the following years as controller were very educational regarding the operations of CBS.

Sunshine in Suburbia

We stayed in the apartment in Richmond Hill, Queens, for almost three years. During that period, Carole and Peter were born in Jamaica Hospital. We visited the 1964 New York World's Fair in Flushing Meadows-Corona Park and explored various parts of Long Island including Jacob Riis Park, the Hamptons, and Montauk Point. Our apartment was walking distance to Holy Child Church, where Carole and Peter were both baptized, and was conveniently located near a large city park. There was a children's playground two minutes away, a large carousel, and a bandshell for outdoor concerts about ten minutes away, where ice cream and picnic food were available. There was a small school across the street with a basketball court, sometimes used for baseball games using a "Spaldeen," a soft rubber ball, and a broomstick handle for a bat. Occasionally a ball would bounce off the front of our house—a sure sign that someone had hit a long home run.

Diagonally across the street was a convenience store; it had a limited selection but carried enough staples to avoid having to go to the supermarket for a quart of milk or a loaf of bread. And there was ample parking on 102nd Street, so our car was always easily accessible. In the heart of Richmond Hill was an old movie theater, an old-fashioned ice cream parlor called Jahns, and Triangle Hofbrau, a Bavarian restaurant that dated back before 1900.

Even though it was a neighborhood filled with families who had lived there for generations, it was beginning to change, as the younger family members began to buy their own homes farther out on Long Island. Likewise, when Carole turned two years old, it was time for us to look for our own home. But where?

Farther out in towns like Roslyn, or Hempstead, or Rockville Centre? Or in Westchester County? New Jersey? Connecticut? It was obvious to Sally and me that we needed to educate ourselves about the pros and cons of these areas. Thus, we began exploring new housing developments all over, from Huntington and Hempstead to Yorktown and Rockland County.

Two people at CBS lived in Connecticut and recommended that I look there; one lived in Riverside, the other in Westport. So, more to humor them, we looked at Riverside and found a perfect small house for our needs. Its only drawback was that it backed up to the New Haven Railroad tracks. Safety was not an issue because of the fencing and shrubbery, and other than the morning and evening rush hours, there were few trains going by.

Apart from the railroad, everything else about the house was positive: lovely street, good neighborhood, close to parks, stores, schools and waterfront. So we made an offer below the asking price. The seller countered slightly higher and said he would not go lower. A negotiating ploy? Perhaps. My Westport friend insisted I talk to his real estate broker, and so more to humor him, since I had no desire to commute such a long distance, I took one Saturday to visit Westport. Sally remained at home with the children since, if I saw something I liked, we would both take more time for revisits.

The first house I saw in Westport was on a cul-de-sac with seven other houses that were built in an old apple orchard. It was twice the house with twice the land that I was seriously negotiating to buy in Riverside. Even though I saw five or six other houses that day, I had the agent take me back to the first one. It was the best of the bunch! I quickly rationalized the distance from New York City by considering the quality of my current commute from Richmond Hill into Manhattan—shorter but less pleasant.

When I had begun commuting in 1961, I would take a short walk to the Jamaica Avenue El into downtown Manhattan. Then I'd switch to a northbound D subway train to Rockefeller Center and walk the ten minutes to my office. The entire trip took up to ninety minutes on an average day—and on the way home, when disembarking from the D train, hundreds of commuters would rush toward one central staircase to get to the Jamaica El. There had to be a better way.

There was: walking nine blocks from the house to catch the 111th Street crosstown bus to the Kew Gardens subway station and riding the E or the F subway train to 53rd Street. Even though I paid a double fare, it cut my commuting time to forty-five minutes. But the subway was always crowded, like the proverbial sardines in a can.

The one-hour train ride from Westport to Grand Central Station put my commute back to ninety minutes, but I could sit in comfort and use the time efficiently. And on another visit to Westport, Sally saw the house, and we agreed that it was for us.

We bought the little chocolate-colored Cape Cod in April 1964 and moved into it in May, shortly before Sally's twenty-eighth and my thirtieth birthdays. I couldn't believe that here I was, not even thirty years old, and I now owned my own house!

That summer we painted the house white, added pine-green shutters and two flower boxes on the upstairs windows, painted the door cranberry red, and added a red bench on the front of the house. My father, recently retired, was a great help painting much of the exterior, something he did very well. One day we were painting the house together, and the postman delivered a letter for him that had been forwarded by my sister. (I was proud that my parents were staying with us in circumstances that were a lot more comfortable than the situation they found when they first arrived in Queens!) It was a letter from my father's supervisor at Worthington Pump, where he had worked for forty years. It was a very complimentary expression of how much my father was appreciated and how he could always be trusted to do a good job. I was so impressed that I later sent copies of the letter to all of our children, as an example to be followed.

Our typical Cape Cod two-story house had two dormers protruding from the sloped roof in the front. The three bedrooms upstairs were not large, but they were sufficient for keeping two adults and four small children very happy for years. The main floor had a living room, dining room, kitchen, family room, half bath, and a screened-in porch. It was a cozy and comfortable place to raise a young family.

Since the house was at the end of the street, the children could play and ride bicycles safely. As an added benefit, our property was shaped like a wide wedge of pie: it was narrow at the street, but 250 feet wide from corner to corner in the rear, providing an ample lawn for all kinds of game playing. Our area of Westport had city water but no sewers. Rather, we had a septic system and a cistern that took care of waste and laundry disposal. The house had been built more than twenty years before and was structurally very sound. The walls were mostly of lath and plaster construction, not the sheetrock so prevalent in modern houses. As a result, it was solid and quiet.

However, the house was not without issues that needed to be addressed. When we connected our washing machine to the external drainpipe and discharged the water, it backed into the basement. We hired our first plumber because of that problem, and when he opened the pipe, he found the drain to the cistern almost entirely clogged with the accumulation of years of soap and grease runoff. Another time, one warm spring day, while cutting the grass with my powered lawn mower, I noticed the wheel go through a wet spot in the lawn. It had not been raining and we had no sprinkler system, so I wondered what could be causing it. Once I smelled it, I knew what it was. (I was wrong, as I found out later.) Our septic system was failing, so we needed professional help again.

Our local septic service arrived with a bright red tank truck and four eager workers. The first man, who did all the talking, was about six feet five inches, with a burly chest and an ample stomach. With his deep bass voice, he said, "All right, Eugene, what's the trouble?" I said, "Follow me."

I turned and led the parade of six to our backyard to the wet spot on the lawn. Walking behind me was Peter, our son, at four years old and three feet high. Then Mr. Six Feet Five. The next three men descended in size from about five feet eight inches to five feet two inches. This was the crew. Their tools included two shovels and a steel probing rod about nine feet long. The biggest and strongest carried nothing. The next two men each carried a shovel and, in reverse logic, the smallest man carried the heaviest and longest piece of equipment.

When we reached the wet spot, we automatically and silently formed a circle around it. One look at the wet spot and Mr. Six Feet Five took action. He pointed to the man with the probing rod, grunted once, and pointed to the wet spot. The little wizened man lifted the steel rod in the air, and like a whaler harpooning a whale, plunged the rod into the soil. In a flash, it slipped beneath our lawn so quickly that our eyes collectively popped and chins hung agog. Mr. Six Feet Five swung his arm in disgust at the little man who'd let the steel bar slip through his fingers. With another grunt, he had the shovel bearers put their blades to work.

No sooner had they shoved the blades into the ground twice, when the ground they were digging fell away from the lawn. We were now staring into a large pit filled with water. After the crew drained the water into the tank truck, we saw the steel probing rod sticking out below. They used a rope and lassoed the steel rod to extricate it from the ooze. Once the water was gone, it revealed a large pit, more than twelve feet deep and five feet wide, lined with fieldstones. This was the cistern, not the septic field as I had thought. Over the years, the same soap scum and fat deposits that had lined the pipes lined its walls. As a result, no water could seep through to the surrounding subsoil. The pit was covered with a cement cap that had cracked and was no longer functional; only a strong layer of grass with its roots tightly knitted together had prevented anything from falling into the cistern.

I shuddered when I realized that if any of our children had jumped up and down on this particular spot, they could have easily disappeared into the water. We were fortunate that the water seepage occurred so the problem could be detected and corrected. As much as we didn't care for the appearance of zoysia grass in our lawn, this was one time we were thankful we had some!

Controller and Vice President of Administration

Shortly after becoming controller of CBS in 1976, I was informed by CBS president Arthur Taylor that I might benefit from attending a financial meeting organized by the Aspen Institute in Berlin, Germany. So, I arranged a two-week trip: one week in Berlin and the following week in Paris. This was the first time that Sally and I had been to Europe, so I arranged for first-class flights on a Pan Am 747. At dinnertime, the flight attendant ushered us to the airplane's upper deck, where a dining room was set up for first-class passengers. We sat at a table with a white tablecloth and fine china. The first course was caviar and vodka, along with a green salad. When dinner was finished, we returned to our seats and slept the rest of the way to Frankfurt Airport, then transferred to a smaller aircraft to fly to Berlin Tempelhof Airport. We stayed at the Kempinski Hotel on the Kurfürstendamm, the West Berlin thoroughfare referred to locally as Ku'damm. From there it was an easy walk to the Reichstag, Brandenburg Gate, and the Tiergarten, and The Berlin Zoo and Park, where, rather than hamburgers and fries, we enjoyed bratwursts and beers.

The difference in atmosphere and activity between East and West Berlin was striking, and the two weeks were exceptional. Attendees at the Aspen meeting included Paul Volcker, president of the Federal Reserve Bank of New York, and John McCloy, the lawyer who was in charge of Germany during the postwar transition period from 1949 to 1952.

Also present were Leonard Silk, PhD and economic writer for *The New York Times,* and the leaders of various German banks as well as representatives from Wall Street. The discussions were about financial concepts I had never heard of before. So I received a crash course in world economics. The Aspen Institute experience was good for me. The meetings were held in a resort near the Wannsee Lake outside of Berlin in the allied zone. Berlin was still a city divided by the Wall, so armed patrol boats were stationed in the Wannsee to prohibit any defectors from using the waterway to escape the Iron Curtain.

There was a small-town exclave located inside the Soviet zone that was connected to Berlin by a narrow strip of land that held a narrow road and railroad track, as a sort of umbilical cord connecting the enclave with the allied sector. On both sides of the strip were wire fences, hundreds of yards of unused land, another fence, and armed guard towers.

As we were driving through this zone, I looked at the sparseness and remarked to the others, "My God, this is no man's land"—at which point one of the German attendees said, "No it's not, it is my *country!*" I felt his pain and regretted making the comment.

∞

As controller, I was responsible for overseeing and evaluating the financial performance of each of the seventeen divisions of CBS.

The largest responsibility was examining the annual budgets of each division, with a major emphasis on requests for capital expenditures. Any major request had to have the approval of the Corporate Board of Directors at an annual meeting in October. In 1976, in anticipation of that meeting, I had prepared a flip card presentation of all the requests that needed board approval for Arthur Taylor to present there.

On the morning of the meeting, I was briefing Taylor on the contents of the cards when he received a call from Paley on his executive line. He told me to wait until he returned from his meeting with Paley, and I could finish the briefing. So I waited in his office with his assistant for close to thirty minutes.

Taylor then returned in an agitated state and asked me to leave. So I went to the office of James Geer, vice president of finance for the corporation, and he asked me how the briefing went. I said, it didn't! Paley called Taylor to his office, and when he returned, he asked me to leave. So we wondered what that meant.

Fifteen minutes later, Taylor's assistant came to inform us that the meeting was canceled. Arthur Taylor was fired! Within the day, John Backe, president of CBS Publishing, would be the new president of CBS.

As controller of the corporation, I had become acquainted with Backe. He did a very good job as head of publishing; he was an Air Force pilot in the Strategic Air Command and a very good leader.

Since he had his own financial people, I wondered if he would keep me as controller. Soon enough, that question was answered. Backe called me into his office and said he had fourteen vice presidents reporting to him and wanted to cut back to only seven.

I would be one of the seven, with the title of vice president of administration. The vice presidents for human resources, buildings and facilities, corporate aircraft, the Ground Floor Restaurant, and the School of Management would report to me.

I said, "John, I understand the other areas, but what is the School of Management?"

Backe said, "Whatever you make it!" When he had worked at General Electric, there was a program for executives to teach them about the businesses GE had and how to handle managing people, and he wanted something similar. So I was faced with the challenge of putting together a program that would give middle managers a taste of CBS businesses, solve problems, and deal with personnel.

I had to find a location, find a school leader, write business problems, and put the school on a planned schedule. I located the school at the New York Institute of Technology. The curriculum was prepared with the help of Sterling Livingston, a professor from Harvard Business School, and CBS executive George Dessart. By all accounts, the school accomplished all that Backe was hoping for. To some of the attendees, it was facetiously referred to as "Jankowski University."

Sadly, neither the school nor John Backe survived when Tom Wyman became president of CBS in 1980. Backe was the first president to carry the chief executive title after William Paley. Unfortunately, Backe began to treat CBS like his corporation and failed to show respect and deference to Paley. But months before Backe was dismissed, he had Paley interview me to be the next president of the Broadcast Group.

∾

William Paley

When people learned that I worked at CBS, quite often they asked, "What was William Paley like?" My contact with Paley spanned twelve years, as I moved through a series of executive positions. Naturally, over time, I developed my own thoughts about the man who built the Columbia Broadcasting System.

William S. Paley (1901–1990) took CBS from a small Philadelphia-based network of radio affiliates to one of the leading radio and television networks in the United States. His father, an immigrant from Ukraine, had settled in Philadelphia and founded what became an extremely successful cigar company. In 1927, when Paley was twenty-seven years old, his father and his business partners bought a Philadelphia-based radio network of sixteen stations called the Columbia Phonographic Broadcasting System to promote the family's cigar brands. With Paley as the advertising manager, the business more than doubled cigar sales within a year, which enabled the family to buy out their partners. They renamed it the Columbia Broadcasting System, and with Paley as chief executive, he expanded the network to 114 affiliate stations within a decade.

Paley changed the broadcast advertising business model by offering programming to the affiliates at a nominal cost, thus offering advertisers and sponsors the widest possible reach. Paley insisted on developing successful, quality programming, and prioritized advertisers and sponsors as the most significant element of the broadcasting equation. The advertisers became the network's primary clients. The affiliates were the distribution system. This model allowed him to build CBS into one of the world's most successful broadcast empires.

To me, Paley was a brilliant, creative charmer who could be warm and funny and enjoy a good joke—but also a hard, decisive, decision-maker, especially with those who reported directly to him!

My earliest meetings with Paley began when I was vice president of administration. In that position, my responsibilities included human resources, worldwide facilities, corporate aircraft (CBS had three: a Gulfstream, a Hawker Siddeley, and a helicopter), the Ground Floor Restaurant on the ground floor of the CBS Building, and the School of Management. My office was on the same floor as Paley's, and at any time he might ask a question about any of those areas.

Then one day Paley called me into his office and his questions were not about any of those concerns. They were about me! He asked about my personal history, family, children, how I began in broadcasting, and other background information. After some pleasant conversation, he said I could leave. Meeting over! A couple of weeks later, another summons, and more talk about me.

After that session, I went to see the president and CEO of CBS, John Backe, and asked what the sessions were about. He merely smiled and said he could not say. It became obvious to me Paley was interviewing me for a job! Then in August of 1977, I became executive vice president of the Broadcast Group with four divisions reporting to me: CBS News, CBS Radio, CBS Television Stations, and CBS Television Network, including entertainment and sports. In turn, I reported to Jack Schneider, president of the Broadcast Group. Then in October, Schneider resigned, and I became president of the Broadcast Group. It was in that position that I began to see Paley on a frequent basis.

CBS held a cocktail reception for me to meet some of the older employees in the Broadcast Group, including some from the West Coast facilities at Television City in Los Angeles. One of them came up to me to congratulate me on my new position. Then he said, "Watch out for the 'PFers.'"

"What's a PFer?" I asked.

"The power fuckers, those people who will approach you and promise anything in return for a favor, i.e., help in a new position, a raise, an on-air position, you name it," he said. "Just don't be surprised when it happens." And it did happen a few times over my career.

At the request of one of our executives, I met with a contestant from the Miss America pageant who wanted to get a part as an actress on a soap opera. During our conversation, she looked very seriously at me and said, "I'm willing to do anything for a part, *anything!*" It became quite clear what she was implying, but I politely told her I did not hire actors. That was the responsibility of the casting directors on the programs, and I did not get involved.

Similar situations arose over the next ten years. And I realized that once one gets seduced, it can only lead to complications that would not be good for the business or for oneself. I was reminded of Lord Acton's warning, "Power tends to corrupt, and absolute power corrupts absolutely." Yet the business world is filled with stories of executives who succumbed to their own peccadillos.

CBS had an executive hotline that allowed executives to call other offices, bypassing secretarial assistants and reaching the individual directly. If I was having a meeting and the exec line rang, and it was Paley asking, "Gene, can you come up?" I would postpone my meeting and report to his office.

I never knew what the topic was until I sat next to Paley's desk. The office reflected the man: it was elegantly decorated with valuable artwork. In his reception area was a George Moore sculpture, and his desk was an antique French gaming table. Sometimes our conversations would cover nonbroadcasting matters, like how he acquired Picasso's 1906 painting *Boy Leading a Horse,* or how he tried to get his wife Barbara ("Babe") Paley to stop smoking, or how he turned his apartment into a hospital wing when she developed lung cancer. Paley told me

Babe was a four-pack-a-day smoker. He had stopped cold turkey when he saw what smoking was doing to his friends. When Jock Whitney, his brother-in-law and best friend, died after a long illness, Paley was devastated.

In July 1978, I was attending a European broadcasters conference with Bill Leonard, a vice president from the Washington office, at the Astir Palace Hotel in Vouliagmeni, Greece, a seaside town outside of Athens. It was during that trip that I asked Leonard to be the president of CBS News.

We had little time to discuss Leonard's new position because I received a phone call from New York requesting that I return as soon as possible. Babe Paley had died, and I was expected to attend her funeral ceremony. And I did. The funeral was held at Christ Episcopal Church in Manhasset, Long Island. Acutely aware of her illness, Mrs. Paley had provided meticulous instructions on how the service and reception afterward should be handled. In effect, she produced her own funeral.

I had met Mrs. Paley at Christmas of 1977, several months before. She attended a party for CBS senior executives, held in the penthouse of a New York hotel. She looked very thin, though she was, as always, dressed beautifully.

∽

When the author Sally Bedell Smith was about to begin a book about Paley, she asked me if she could interview me at some future time. I said absolutely. She never called! After her book, *In All His Glory: The Life and Times of William S. Paley: The Legendary Tycoon and His Brilliant Circle*, came out in 1990, it was obvious she had already drawn her conclusions about him and knew I wouldn't support her thesis. All the quotes she used were from people who did not like the man. Bad journalism!

President, CBS Broadcast Group: The Early Years

When I became president of the CBS Broadcast Group in 1977, the prime-time schedule was in third place, far behind ABC and NBC. It was our main objective to change that ranking in as short a time as possible. Management was not happy, the affiliates were not happy, and the shareholders, I assume, were not happy.

Despite the poor performance of the entertainment schedule, the shining light of the network was CBS News. The *CBS Evening News* with Walter Cronkite and *60 Minutes* with correspondents Mike Wallace, Harry Reasoner, Morley Safer, Dan Rather, and Ed Bradley were standouts in an otherwise poor showing during the weekly broadcasts. The prime-time ratings began to cause unease among the more than 200 affiliated stations. This uneasiness had to be addressed!

When I took over management of the Broadcast operation, I was a stranger to the affiliates. So was Bob Daly, who came out of Business Affairs to become president of Entertainment Programming. Newly named network president James Rosenfield, formerly a sales executive, was a somewhat familiar face; he was responsible for sales and affiliate relations. We needed to win over the affiliates as quickly as possible to prevent defections to other networks.

To address that problem, we went to Mr. Paley and asked if he would attend our next affiliate board meeting. He seldom went to such sessions, feeling no need to. But to show his support for the new management team, he attended the meeting in November 1977 in Key Largo, Florida. His presence not only demonstrated his faith in us, it helped placate any unease among the station owners. The stations were always important to Paley. He knew their values. It is why he honored our request to attend the meeting.

At dinner, I asked Tom Chauncey, owner of KOOL TV in Phoenix, to what he attributed his success. Without missing a beat, he pointed to William Paley and said, "I just do anything he tells me." And then he added, "Because I had a chance to meet you new fellows, tomorrow I'm buying 50,000 shares of CBS stock." When I saw him every year after that, he was always pleased about his investment!

One strength the major networks have always had is distribution. With one purchase, an advertiser has the ability to reach 100 percent of the television homes. Willian Paley understood that. When he was building CBS, he traveled the country to sign affiliation agreements with individual stations and group owners. Over time, CBS had some of the best stations—the largest markets in the country.

∽

That affiliate board meeting in Key Largo in 1977 was memorable for other reasons as well. Back in New York City, Walter Cronkite was working to put together an international meeting, by satellite, between President Anwar Sadat of Egypt and Prime Minister Menachim Begin of Israel.

CBS made it happen. On November 14, CBS broadcast a live interview with Cronkite in New York, Sadat in Cairo, and Begin in Tel Aviv. It was during that broadcast that Sadat and Begin agreed to have further discussions about peace in the Middle East. Those discussions ultimately resulted in Sadat and Begin receiving the Nobel Peace Prize in 1978, for jointly having negotiated peace between Egypt and Israel. As the first live international broadcast between world leaders, the program showed the promise of the good that can come from improved communications.

If prejudice is primarily due to ignorance, then programs designed to educate and inform the general public should be a great way to build a path to better understanding among the people of the world. Sadly, I do not believe that that has happened. All of the advances in electronic communications, while making people more aware of problems in the world, has not helped resolve those problems. It is not technology that solves problems; it is people willing to address difficult issues and seek acceptable solutions that are needed to help resolve serious issues.

Once again, this is a reminder that technology has no native land. It is neither good nor bad; it is but a tool that can be used to help or hinder progress toward peace.

∽

The year 1977 was a remarkable year in history and in my career. One could say that my first year as the president of the Broadcast Group was a trial by fire, which required me to not only succeed in the job but to respond to world events, represent

CBS on the global stage, celebrate its legacy, protect the legacy of film and of sports, and more.

But first, a call from the White House.

I had no sooner walked into our house in Weston after my commute when Sally said bluntly:

"The White House called!"

"The White House? As in 1600 Pennsylvania Avenue?"

"Yes. That White House. Here is the phone number."

Why would the White House be calling me? I was new in my position as president. Was it something CBS News said? The politicians in Washington never did like the major networks. They always felt that they had too much power. In truth, they did not like the fact that the broadcasters could communicate directly with the people—and sometimes the news did not favor their political agenda.

In 1971, CBS had broadcast a one-hour prime-time documentary called *The Selling of the Pentagon* that had created a furor in Washington—so much so that Frank Stanton, the president of CBS at the time, was asked to testify before the House Committee on Interstate and Foreign Commerce's Subcommittee on Special Investigations. He did, and as is so often true, the facts of the program could not be disputed.

The call was from Rep. Harley O. Staggers of West Virginia, chairman of the very same House committee. With more curiosity than concern, I dialed the number. I had never met Rep. Staggers and was confident that CBS had done nothing to cause any problem with him or his constituency.

"Mr. Jankowski, I want you to be the grand marshal of the Elkins, West Virginia, Mountain State Forest Festival this fall. It is a major event, and I believe CBS could benefit from your participation."

Well, I thought, if I want to build better relationships with members of Congress, this might be an interesting way to begin.

So I accepted.

Sally could not go with me, so I decided to take my two youngest daughters, Judy and Jennifer. It could be an educational experience for them. We would take the CBS plane and fly directly to Elkins, arriving late afternoon on a Friday in time for dinner and a speech. Then I would serve as grand marshal of the parade on Saturday morning, we'd watch the mountaineering competitions on Saturday afternoon, and return home Sunday.

On the flight to Elkins, a strong weather front moved into the mountainous region. The fog was so thick, the airport was closed! Luckily, there was another airfield about fifteen miles away. The pilots changed the flight plan and also left a message with the team in Elkins. They went to work! When we landed, we were met by West Virginia state troopers who said, "Get in the back seat and hold on!"

So I sat in the middle and held one daughter on each side of me. The trooper put on his flasher, turned on his siren, and away we went, as fast as the winding roads would allow. As it was getting dark and foggy, it was slightly hair-raising. But in the midst of our speeding trip, the girls yelled gleefully, "Whee, just like the *Dukes of Hazzard*!"

And as if in a TV sitcom, we arrived just as the party was about to begin!

The next morning, a large Cadillac convertible with my name on the side door in bold letters, GENE JANKOWSKI CBS, transported us to the parade site. Harley Staggers led the parade in a vintage automobile, Senator Jennings Randolph was in the next car. Then, a Cadillac convertible with Jennifer, Judy, and me. Crowds were on both sides of the narrow street, waving and cheering. I noticed that one woman started applauding and cheering as my convertible passed by.

I heard her male companion ask, "Why are you cheering? Who is Gene Jankowski?"

She said, "I don't know, but he's from CBS!"

Humbling, to say the least! But it was another reminder that any adulation I might receive in the years ahead would most likely be due to my position and not for me personally.

∽

Just before I stepped into the role of president, the CBS Sports department had orchestrated "The Heavyweight Championship of Tennis," a series of high-profile tennis matches pitting the reigning world champion, Jimmy Connors, against a series of opponents, including Rod Laver, John Newcombe, Manuel Orantes, and Ilie Nastase. The matches were advertised as "winner take all," with a pot of $250,000.

But there was a catch. The whole thing was a sham. In Connors's match against Nastase, CBS had guaranteed Connors $500,000, win or lose, and Nastase had been guaranteed $150,000. When the truth came to light, the Federal Communications Commission (FCC) launched an investigation, threatening to revoke the licenses of all the CBS local television stations for misleading the public.

Talk about a trial by fire! On my very first day as president, I was thrust into the middle of this PR crisis. I didn't have any connections at the FCC, and they certainly didn't know me. To bridge the gap, we set up a series of meetings. Unfortunately, with the investigation underway, our lips were sealed on the tennis match debacle.

So, what could I do? I talked about myself, my values, and what CBS stood for. I also took decisive action, firing the president of CBS Sports and penalizing his assistant. Then, I stepped in front of the camera, on a Sunday afternoon during our sports programming, to apologize to the American people.

"For over fifty years," I began, "CBS has strived to uphold

the principle that our broadcasts must be truthful. I regret to say that in four tennis broadcasts, this was not the case."

I went on to explain the deceptive "winner-take-all" setup, acknowledging our failure to disclose the financial arrangements with the players. I emphasized that the integrity of the matches themselves was never in question, but the way we presented them was undeniably misleading.

The most crucial line of my apology? "Integrity is our most important possession."

CBS's reputation for trustworthiness was paramount to its success. It was a key factor in attracting advertisers and talent and maintaining positive relationships with both Congress and Wall Street. This commitment to integrity was even a driving force behind newscaster Walter Cronkite's status as "the most trusted man in America."

William Paley understood the immense power of broadcasting. He championed fair and balanced news, and believed in presenting the facts, then letting the audience form their own conclusions.

Looking back, I wish my first network television appearance had been under more favorable circumstances. But the experience taught me a valuable lesson about the importance of transparency and accountability.

Because of the steps we took, CBS received a reprimand from the FCC, but didn't lose any of its stations. And I forged valuable connections with the FCC commissioners. It was indeed a trial by fire, but one that ultimately strengthened CBS and prepared me for the challenges ahead.

∽

CBS 50th Anniversary Special

Those first few years as president of CBS Broadcasting were filled with highs and lows. This was a high. In 1977, CBS celebrated its fiftieth anniversary, using the date of September 18, 1927, when the Columbia Phonographic Broadcasting System went on air as its "birthdate."

Perhaps prompted by NBC's celebration of its fiftieth anniversary in 1976, Paley and CBS wanted to put on a real showstopper. We hired Alexander Cohen, a Broadway producer who had brought the Tony Awards to TV, as producer, and his talented wife, Hildy Parks, as writer. With just four months to pull it all together, it was decided that the tribute would consist of seven consecutive nights of programming that would bring together 100 network stars, past, present, and future, with Walter Cronkite and Mary Tyler Moore as hosts. Cohen wanted all of the luminaries to attend a taping at Television City in Los Angeles dressed in formal tuxedos and gowns.

Contacting all the talent was an exceptionally long and arduous process. I asked Cohen if he was succeeding in reaching his objective. He said it was going well; most stars were happy to be part of the process. Except for one: Red Skelton, the star of *The Red Skelton Show*, a popular comedy/variety show that aired from 1951 to 1971. Cohen said that every time he called Skelton, Red would say, "Demographics!" and hang up. His program had been canceled by CBS because the audience was much older than the desired advertising audience, and the sales department could no longer get high enough ad rates to cover the cost of production. Furthermore, when it was time to renew the contract, Red Skelton wanted even more money. Even though the program had a respectable share of the audience, it still lost money and would lose even more if the network agreed to his wishes. So the show was canceled, citing "demographics" as the cause.

I asked Cohen for Skelton's phone number and left a message with his assistant. Days later, when I was attending an affiliate conference in Arizona, I was paged: it was Red Skelton returning my call. I said, "Mr. Skelton, I am the president of CBS Broadcasting, and we are doing an anniversary special on the history of CBS." He said, "I know of it, but I am busy doing other things."

I said, "Mr. Skelton, we will be taking a photograph of all the stars who worked for CBS. You may remember a photograph taken by MGM for their twenty-fifth anniversary." He said, "Yes, I am in that picture." So I said, "Well, you could be one of the few stars to be in both photos, perhaps the only one, and it would be a shame if you were not in the CBS picture."

He said, "Well, I'll think about it." We finished the call, and a few days later, Cohen called me and said Skelton was going to show up.

When Skelton arrived at Television City, it was like old home week. He walked in with a big grin and received a warm welcome from stagehands who remembered him fondly. It was one of the highlights of a long, arduous day. For me, it was a crash course in the history of CBS, and the stars who brought entertainment and information into our homes over the years.

Two "Matt Dillons" were there; James Arness, who played the role in *Gunsmoke* for twenty years, and William Conrad, who played the role on the radio. (He also later starred in *Jake and the Fatman* on CBS television.) When the show wrapped and people were leaving, I had the opportunity to thank many of them personally for their contributions to CBS. I especially enjoyed meeting Roy Rogers, one of my boyhood heroes from Saturday afternoon movie matinees and later on television. I also confirmed that Arness was really six feet seven inches tall!

∽

Kennedy Center Honors

In the fall of 1977, Bob Daly, the president of CBS Entertainment, called to tell me he had had a meeting with producer George Stevens Jr., son of the famous Hollywood director George Stevens, on behalf of the John F. Kennedy Center for the Performing Arts in Washington, DC. The center planned to create an annual awards gala to honor five individuals who had a nationally recognized career in the performing arts for their contributions to American culture. Stevens would be the producer of the program.

Daly and I agreed that a special of this kind would not have a large television audience, but it would be a great public relations image builder for CBS. It had all the potential of being a high-quality cultural event. The evening, hosted by Leonard Bernstein, would provide an opportunity for stars of Hollywood to mingle with politicians from Washington. The first five honorees in December 1978 were Marian Anderson, Fred Astaire, George Balanchine, Richard Rodgers, and Arthur Rubenstein.

Over the years, I always found it fascinating to watch how bold-faced names in Washington could be enamored of bold-faced names from Hollywood and vice versa. More than forty years later, the Kennedy Center Honors continues to be a part of the CBS television schedule every December. The Honors is more than just a TV special; it is an entire weekend, which begins on Saturday evening with a dinner at the State Department, where the recipients are honored by the Secretary of State. On Sunday morning, there is a brunch at which visiting dignitaries have an opportunity to mingle with Hollywood and Washington celebrities. Then, on Sunday afternoon, the honorees are welcomed at the White House, where the President of the United States officially presents them with their medals. That evening, the recipients attend a formal performance at the Kennedy Center, where each awardee is honored with a series of tributes. The stage performance is then followed by a late dinner in the halls of the Kennedy Center.

Up until then, the award had always been given to five individuals. In 1985, Broadway lyricist Alan Lerner was to be honored. But actress and TV personality Kitty Carlisle Hart called me to complain that recognizing Lerner and not Frederick Loewe, the composer with whom Lerner created his most successful musicals, including *Brigadoon* and *My Fair Lady*, would be a travesty. Both should be honored. So Hart lobbied me and the team at the Kennedy Center and succeeded in her quest.

For some reason, Lerner and Loewe were not talking to each other. But the night of the performance, they shook hands in the presidential box, to the cheers of the audience. A night to remember. By any standard, the Kennedy Center Honors continues to deliver everything Daly and I thought it would, forty-eight years ago.

∽

Meeting George Lucas

When the motion picture *Star Wars* was released in 1977, it was a megahit at the box office. I decided I wanted to meet the producer, George Lucas. Lucas lived in San Francisco, so I arranged to have lunch with him on a business trip to the "city by the Bay." I was hoping there might be a way to interest Lucas in producing a television program.

Lucas insisted we meet in my room at the Stanford Court Hotel, where he had milk and a sandwich. He then proceeded to tell me why he felt *Star Wars* was such a smash hit. He had a master plan for the "Skywalker Saga," a series of sequels, even before the first movie was produced. Lucas said he had planned on a movie that would be produced for about $9 million, generate at least $18 million at the box office, and he would keep 30 percent of the gross.

I asked Lucas if there was any key decision he had made to help *Star Wars* be so successful. He said, "Designing the princess: should she be 'James Bond-ish' or 'Walt Disney-ish'?" In deference to his mother, he had gone with "Walt Disney-ish." As a result, he knew of one boy who had seen the movie forty-six times. It is repeat sales that make for such huge grosses. Also, Lucas said that he had produced the movie for a television viewer's habits. By that he meant that traditional motion pictures took about fifteen minutes to get the viewer absorbed in the story. He had planned action immediately after the credits that had the audience on the "edge of their seats" before they even knew who were the "good guys" or the "bad guys."

Furthermore, Lucas wanted to be able to merchandise some of the characters. Hence, about seven out of the ten characters were creatures created for that purpose.

All in all, a brilliant plan for a series of blockbuster motion pictures.

As far as Lucas doing television for CBS, I struck out. Perhaps in years to come, but right then, the movies were demanding all of his attention.

Out of the success of *Star Wars*, Lucas had grown his special effects company, Industrial Light & Magic, that to this day creates some of the most stunning visual effects in motion pictures and television.

For all his success in the motion picture industry, Lucas was presented with the American Film Institute Lifetime Achievement Award in 2005.

Over the years, I was able to visit with George at his Skywalker Ranch in Marin County, California. Always the gracious host, he proudly showed me his office, studios, theater, vineyards, and art collection. I never did get him to produce any program for CBS!

∞

Whenever I was in Los Angeles, I would stay at the Beverly Hills Hotel. I felt it was a convenient location for any meetings I might have. Also, it was William Paley's favorite place to stay. On the rare occasions when we were there at the same time, it offered an opportunity to discuss business casually.

One day in 1979, I was in LA and Paley was in New York, and my phone rang. It was Paley calling to tell me about a meeting he had had with Donald J. Hall, Sr., the chairman and president of Hallmark Cards. He told me that Hall was disappointed in the way the *Hallmark Hall of Fame,* a series of specials that had been on the air with NBC since 1952, was being treated by Fred Silverman, the president at NBC. Would CBS be interested in broadcasting the Hallmark specials?

I was scheduled to return to New York the following day, so I said it would be easy to stop at the Hallmark headquarters in Kansas City on my way back. The next day I flew to Kansas City and met with Don Hall, a most gracious host. He gave me a tour of the Hallmark facilities, including a penthouse suite he referred to as the "Eisenhower apartment," intended to host important guests. The first guest to stay in the suite had been Dwight D. Eisenhower. After a few hours, I left Hallmark for my flight to New York.

CBS agreed to carry the *Hallmark Hall of Fame,* and began the 1979 season with a broadcast of *All Quiet on the Western Front* featuring the actor Richard Thomas. We held a special screening in the Kennedy Center, an impressive beginning to a new relationship. For the next twenty years, I received a Christmas ornament from Don Hall, especially created for his business friends.

∽

American Film Institute

Ever since working with George Stevens, Jr., on the Kennedy Center Honors, shortly after becoming president of CBS in 1977, he and I had become friendly. In 1978, I received a call from Stevens in his capacity as founding director and chief executive of the American Film Institute. When we met in my office, he asked me if I would become a director of the AFI Conservatory, an accredited graduate school located in Los Angeles. I said yes, and today I am still associated with the AFI. For four years, I also served as chairman of the board of this fine institution. What an honor for that nine-year-old boy from Buffalo who fell in love with moving pictures!

Since its inception, the AFI has had only three chief executives: George Stevens Jr., Jean Picker Firstenberg, and now, Robert Gazzale. Each of them has seen the AFI grow in importance. Today, the AFI Conservatory is recognized as one of the best film schools in the country.

During my association with the organization, I have had the opportunity to meet many talented actors like Charlton Heston, Clint Eastwood, Steve Martin, Diane Keaton, Morgan Freeman, Gregory Peck, Audrey Hepburn, Sidney Poitier, Kirk Douglas, and directors Steven Spielberg and Martin Scorsese. My love for the moving image resulted in many extraordinary events and associations. In 1989, the AFI celebrated its twenty-fifth anniversary with a gala called "Back to the Rose Garden." The name referred to the Rose Garden at the White House, where in 1965 President Lyndon B. Johnson announced the creation of an institute devoted to educating and inspiring students of American film.

A formal dinner in Washington brought together luminaries from Hollywood and the political arena. David Wolper, the renowned television and film producer, directed the entertainment for the evening. He had various celebrities recite famous lines from motion pictures: "Frankly, my dear, I don't give a damn" (*Gone with the Wind*), "You're gonna need a bigger boat" (*Jaws*), and "Toto, I've a feeling we're not in Kansas anymore" (*The Wizard of Oz*) were just a few examples.

Wolper had President George H.W. Bush point to his wife, Barbara, and say, "Here's looking at you, kid." Bush delivered the unforgettable line from the 1942 film *Casablanca*, spoken by actor Humphrey Bogart to actress Ingrid Bergman, flawlessly, to great applause. A memorable moment in the history of the AFI.

My father, Walter Kasmier Jankowski, in Buffalo, New York, in 1935, building our garage. What he lacked in terms of formal schooling, he more than made up for by having an innate sense of curiosity and craftsmanship. Best of all, he was a loving husband and a caring father.

With my parents, Walter and Marie-Theresa Jankowski, upon my graduation from Canisius College in Buffalo in 1955.

Jacksonville Beach, Florida, 1956. After attending Navy Officer Candidate School, my first assignment was to aviation ground officer school at the Naval Air Training Center in Jacksonville. A Buffalo boy, I was pretty excited about the warm weather and proximity to the beach!

My time in the Navy was a growth experience. As a young officer, I was given major responsibilities over people, materiel, and missions. This training served me well in management positions in my civilian career.

My office at 51 West 52nd Street in Manhattan, known as Black Rock. I was one of the first inhabitants of the building, designed by Eero Saarinen and completed in 1964. My office as president of the CBS Broadcast Group was on the thirty-fourth floor, one below the office of legendary CEO William S. Paley.

When I became president of the CBS Broadcast Group in 1977, the lineup of journalists and producers at CBS News was unbeatable. The *CBS Evening News* was the number-one evening news program for decades; *60 Minutes* and *Face the Nation* were other outstanding broadcasts. During my tenure we launched *CBS Sunday Morning* and *48 Hours*, which remain on the air today.

Arthur Godfrey was one of the biggest stars in television and radio during the 1950s and 1960s. It was not until I got to know him personally that I realized what an excellent salesman he was. As a result, I organized for him to give a presentation to the CBS sales staff. Godfrey hosted us at his farm in Paeonian Springs, Virginia, and even manned the barbecue!

With Bob Daly, president of CBS Entertainment, and Oscar Katz, vice president of Programming. Daly and I realized that the CBS entertainment headquarters should move to Los Angeles from New York. CBS's "Television City" studios in LA produced a series of hit shows on the network in the 1980s and 1990s.

The *CBS 50th Anniversary Special* was one of the first challenges of my tenure as President of the CBS Broadcast Group. CBS wanted to put on a real showstopper, but corralling all of the network's biggest stars into one room was quite an ordeal! In the end it was a memorable and star-studded event hosted by Walter Cronkite and Mary Tyler Moore, and a success for the network.

Bottom, from left: Lassie, Jean Stapleton, Walter Cronkite, Alfred Hitchcock, Mary Tyler Moore, Ellen Corby, Gene Rayburn; second row: Vivian Vance, Milburn Stone, Ann Sothern, Barbara Bain; third row: Nancy Walker, George Burns, Cicely Tyson, Arthur Godfrey, Red Skelton; fourth row: Gale Storm, Danny Kaye, Sandy Duncan, Telly Savalas, Dale Evans, Roy Rogers, Ken Murray; fifth row: Eric Scott, Cami Cotler, Bonnie Franklin, William Conrad, Eva Gabor, Allen Funt, Jim Conway, Doug Thomas, Bob Keeshan; sixth row: Dennis Weaver, Ray Walston, Sally Struthers, Garry Moore, Linda Lavin, Douglas Edwards, Betty White, Bob Schieffer, Ned Beatty, Charles Kuralt; seventh row: Arlene Francis, Jamie Farr, Adrienne Barbeau, Vicki Lawrence, Mary McDonough, Don Knotts, Lucille Ball, Ed Asner, Jackie Cooper, Esther Rolle, Joan Hackett, Eric Sevareid; eighth row: Mike Wallace, Michael Learned, Sherman Hemsley, Jack Whitaker, Isabel Sanford, Judy Norton Taylor, Bob Denver, Carroll O'Connor, Dwayne Hickman, Richard Hottelet, Will Geer, Lesley Stahl, Art Carney, Tony Randall, Bob Newhart; ninth row: Dick Smothers, Hughes Rudd, Ted Knight, Georgia Engel, John Walmsley, Charles Collingwood, Valerie Harper, Julie Kavner, David Harper, Bill Macy, Ken Berry; tenth row: Art Linkletter, Glen Campbell, Buddy Ebsen, Michael Learned, John Forsythe, Steve Allen, Carol Burnett, Jim Nabors, Bea Arthur, Loretta Swit, Ed Bradley, Andy Griffith, Lee Meriwether, Demond Wilson, Lynda Carter, James Arness; top row: Dick Van Dyke, Jack Lord, Ralph Waite, Bernard Kalb, Martin Landau, Rob Reiner, Lynnie Greene, John Amos, Bob Barker, Bert Convy, Dan Rather, Richard Crenna, Mike Connors, David Groh.

With Red Skelton and Carroll O'Connor at the CBS 50th Anniversary celebration. Red Skelton threatened not to show until at the last minute I convinced him to attend!

With George Stevens, Jr., founding producer of the Kennedy Center Honors, and screen legend Cary Grant at an event for the Honors. Grant was an honoree in 1981. CBS broadcast this esteemed ceremony for many years, which still takes place annually nearly 50 years after its inception in 1978.

With actress Cicely Tyson at an event for the Kennedy Center Honors. Tyson was an honoree in 2015.

With longtime *CBS Evening News* anchor Walter Cronkite, at the US Open in Flushing Meadows, New York. During his tenure, Cronkite was dubbed "the most trusted man in television."

My daughter Carol, at the time a Georgetown student, aboard the Wyntje, with Cronkite at the helm.

With future president George H.W. Bush at the Daytona 500, broadcast on CBS Sports.

I was honored with the "Good Scout Award" by the Boy Scouts of America in 1983. Former football coach and CBS broadcaster John Madden presented me with the award. I loved participating in the Boy Scouts when I was growing up.

I received the Humanitarian Award from the National Conference of Christians and Jews entertainment division in 1985. Actor Danny Kaye, the first recipient of the award, presented me with the award.

I was fortunate enough to meet Pope John Paul II with my wife, Sally, at the Vatican. I also met Pope Francis, as well as a number of US presidents and international dignitaries.

CJ the orangutan was a surprise TV star in the 1980s, featured on *The Love Boat*, *TJ Hooker*, and *Mr. Smith*. He also appeared in two Clint Eastwood films. Somehow, I resisted his advances!

A hug from Diane Sawyer, on the other hand, was impossible to resist. Sawyer joined CBS News as a reporter in 1978, co-anchored the *CBS Morning News* and the *CBS Early Morning News* before being named the first female correspondent on 60 Minutes in 1984. We became friendly over the years. Diane and Lesley Stahl are two of the best journalists of my era. CBS never should have let Sawyer go to ABC.

With actress Angela Lansbury, star of the long-running CBS hit series
Murder, She Wrote.

I consider myself lucky to have known and worked for CBS founder and CEO William S. Paley, who in many ways shaped the 20th-century media landscape. Here are the two of us at my retirement party from CBS in 1989.

My professional and personal lives often intermingled, especially when my wife
Sally and I hosted parties at our apartment on Fifth Avenue. Here I am in the
1990s with long-time *CBS Evening News* anchor Dan Rather, and business woman
and media personality Martha Stewart, whom I met when we both lived in
Westport, Connecticut.

Sally and me with our children, Judith, Jennifer, Carole, and Peter. The kids and I were devastated when Sally died of cancer in 2007.

My wedding to Lisa Hayes in August 2009 at Holy Trinity Church in Georgetown, DC. We had both lost our spouses in the previous few years, and our meeting and marriage has brought sixteen years of happiness to both of us.

A memorable dinner on Nantucket with my wife, Lisa, former football player and media personality Frank Gifford, his wife, TV host Kathie Lee Gifford, their daughter, Cassidy, and a friend in 2013. I met Gifford at CBS Radio in the 1960s, and we remained friends until his death in 2015.

Lisa and me with my children, their spouses, and my grandchildren at the
Hartwood Club in New York: Carole and Aquiles Suarez and their daughters Sara
and Julia; Peter and Linda Jankowski with sons Sam and Luke; Judith and Charles
Lyons with Maria and Mark; and Jennifer and Geoffrey Odlum with sons Geoffrey,
Patrick, and Thomas. (After this photo, my grandson Geoffrey married Elsa, and
they are expecting a baby as of this writing; and Patrick is engaged to Sophie.)

CBS News

T he quality of an organization depends on the quality of its people, and CBS News has always had some of the best. The outstanding men and women at CBS News helped build a trusted news division with a quality image.

When I became president of the CBS Broadcast Group, the lineup of journalists and producers at CBS News was impressive, including Walter Cronkite, Dan Rather, Roger Mudd, Charles Collingwood, Charles Kuralt, Mike Wallace, Harry Reasoner, Eric Sevareid, Morley Safer, Richard Hottelet, Winston Burdett, Tom Fenton, Perry Wolf, Joe Wershba, Don Hewitt, Bill Plante, Van Gordon Sauter, Bill Leonard, Diane Sawyer, Lesley Stahl, Steve Kroft, and Bernard Kalb. They carried on the tradition of excellence established by Doug Edwards, Robert Trout, Ed Murrow, William Shirer, Dallas Townsend, and others.

60 Minutes was another outstanding broadcast, with a roster of journalists like Mike Wallace, Harry Reasoner, Morley Safer, Lesley Stahl, Dan Rather, Diane Sawyer, Ed Bradley, Steve Kroft, and commentary by Andy Rooney. With executive producer Don Hewitt, this talented team contributed to the program's longevity over more than fifty years. The network will never see anything like it again.

∽

CBS Sunday Morning

Protecting the CBS News image and the quality of its work was an honor and a big responsibility. When I asked Bill Leonard to be president of CBS News in 1978, he agreed, but emphasized the need to address the Sunday morning programming. At that time, CBS was producing two programs with the guidance of the Council of Churches: *Look Up and Live* and *Lamp Unto My Feet.* Out of more than two hundred affiliated stations, only about twenty carried these programs each Sunday. Clearly, something needed to change.

Leonard proposed producing a ninety-minute program leading into *Face the Nation,* the successful Sunday news interview program. The first challenge was reclaiming the time slots from the Council of Churches without generating negative publicity for CBS. We held several meetings with church leaders to convince them that programs with low viewership should not be produced. I explained that the new news program would include relevant stories on religion, and it was up to them to provide us with stories that would have broad appeal.

Once we recaptured the time period, the focus shifted to producing a ninety-minute news program that was "softer" than the nightly hard news broadcasts. Leonard envisioned it as akin to leisurely reading the feature sections of a Sunday newspaper.

The next hurdle was getting the affiliated TV stations to agree to carry what we believed would be a unique and informative program. It would begin at 10 a.m. East Coast time, leading into *Face the Nation* at 11:30 a.m., creating a two-hour block of news and information.

When we presented the concept to our affiliate board, they liked the program, but not the time period. One of our affiliated stations was airing a very profitable movie from 10 a.m. to 12 p.m. We asked if they would carry our program if we changed the broadcast time to 9 a.m. to 10:30 a.m., and they agreed. That is why *Sunday Morning* now airs at 9 a.m. instead of 10 a.m. East Coast time.

Sunday Morning became a critical and financial success for CBS, with anchors changing from Charles Kuralt to Charles Osgood to Jane Pauley. The program continues to perform well into its fortieth year. I am proud of the part I played in getting that program on the air.

∽

CBS News/London Bureau

The CBS News Bureau in London was once located near the Hyde Park Hotel, close to Hyde Park and Harrods department store. In 1980, when the bureau was established, we decided to invite Prime Minister Margaret Thatcher to attend the dedication ceremony.

The bureau was to be named in honor of Edward R. Murrow, the CBS correspondent who did a remarkable job reporting from London during World War II. Thatcher was honored to be invited, as she knew it was Murrow's reporting that had brought England's plight to the attention of millions of Americans.

Bill Leonard and I went outside to welcome Thatcher at the appointed time. Two Jaguars arrived, one with her security detail and one with the prime minister.

After a tour of the bureau, Thatcher made some gracious remarks about how much Murrow's work was appreciated by the

British people. At the conclusion of her comments, she had to leave, so Leonard and I escorted her to her automobile. A quick goodbye, and she was gone. No huge fanfare! Just two cars. No ambulance, no medical technicians, no press corps, no armored vehicles. Despite her reputation as the "Iron Lady," in person Thatcher was low-key and very heartwarming. I commented to Leonard that I felt like we just had a visit from a grandmother!

∞

Walter Cronkite

"I must go down to the seas again, to the lonely sea and the sky,
    And all I ask is a tall ship and a star to steer her by."
These lines from a 1902 poem by John Masefield were recited by William Horbach, a sailing friend of Walter Cronkite's, at a funeral ceremony for Cronkite in St. Bartholomew's Church in Manhattan on July 23, 2009.

Besides being an outstanding journalist with the reputation as the "most trusted man in America," Walter was a very accomplished sailor. I experienced his nautical skills in 1981, when he called to invite me to join him on a sail in Nassau, Bahamas. I said yes, if I could bring my daughter Carole and her friend Nancy Park. "Georgetown students would be welcome. Absolutely," Walter said.

So the three of us flew to Nassau and went sailing with Walter and his wife, Betsy. It was a memorable afternoon. As he raised the sail, Walter referred to the actor Errol Flynn, also a sailor, who was rumored to have died in the arms of an eighteen-year-old girl. He said, "What a way to go. On an eighty-foot boat in the arms of an eighteen-year-old girl."

Quick-witted Betsy responded by saying, "Walter, with

your luck, it will be on an eighteen-foot boat in the arms of an eighty-year-old woman!"

Betsy was great! She once was asked what Walter worried about. "Shrinking," was the recorded response.

Cronkite kept his boat, Wyntje, anchored in Edgartown, Massachusetts, where he had a cottage. He loved to sail his boat toward a restaurant on the harbor. As the diners watched his boat coming toward them, he would do a hard tack to port and watch their jaws drop!

Walter was a major contributor to the image of CBS as the "Tiffany Network." His credibility was above the norm. When he made negative comments about the United States involvement in Vietnam, President Lyndon B. Johnson allegedly said, "If I have lost Cronkite, I have lost the support for the war."

∽

Dan Rather

When Cronkite said he wanted to leave the anchor position at *CBS Evening News*, I knew we would have a difficult problem to address. By 1981, he made it clear to news management that he wanted to step down. He had been at the chair since 1962. Eventually, management agreed to his request, and the search for his successor began. Replacing the "most trusted man in America" was no easy task.

The former president of CBS News, Dick Salant, had strongly hinted to Roger Mudd that he would be the heir apparent. Mudd *had* frequently filled in for Cronkite when he was on vacation. But neither the current president, Bill Leonard, nor I felt that Mudd was the best fit for this crucial role.

The *Evening News* and its anchorperson are the "front page" of CBS News, and to a large extent, they shape the image of all of CBS. It's more than just presentation. Besides being a credible journalist, the anchor also has to be a goodwill ambassador for the company, meeting with station owners, the press, and occasionally members of the advertising community.

After careful consideration, I believed that Dan Rather would be the ideal choice. He was an experienced journalist, well-traveled to global hotspots, had served as a White House correspondent, understood Washington politics, and possessed a genuine charm in face-to-face interactions with both established and new station owners. His good looks were also a significant asset for the anchor position. Bill Leonard agreed that Rather was the man for the job.

However, Roone Arledge, the president of ABC News, also recognized Rather's potential, and was working hard to improve the image and competitiveness of ABC News. When we began negotiating with Rather for the position, ABC made a serious effort to lure him away to be the anchorman of their evening news program. I met personally with Rather to persuade him that his best career move would be to stay with CBS. He had a history with the company, knew the people, and had earned their respect. I also strongly believed that with Rather as Cronkite's replacement, he would increase viewership for the program and be a strong competitor among the other news programs—and I told him so!

To his credit, Rather gave serious consideration to my argument, while also listening to the proposal from ABC. Enter Richard Leibner, agent par excellence! Leibner represented many local and network news stars and had been Rather's agent for several years. He was exceptional at his work.

Eventually, all of our discussions came down to money. How much and for how long? Leonard and I agreed that we would probably have to settle for a figure above $1 million a year. We were not prepared when Leibner said it would be at least $6 million a year, over five years! We asked Leibner if we agreed to an amount, did we have a deal?

Leibner said yes, but with a figure that large, I would have to get approval from the corporation, since it was an amount larger than the profits of some of the smaller CBS divisions. So I went to John Backe, president and CEO of the CBS Corporation, with the proposal. He flatly refused! There was no way he was going to allow any CBS employee to be paid that much.

I tried to be as persuasive as I could with Backe, stressing the importance of Rather to the future of CBS and the cost to the company if we lost him to ABC. Backe was adamant in his position. Disappointed, I left his office and called Bill Leonard to report my failure with Backe.

What to do? Leonard made a proposal that required my approval. He suggested he do something I could not do: He would go over Backe's head and call William Paley directly. He had known Paley for years and was willing to risk any backlash from Backe, as he was ready for retirement anyhow. He would ask for a meeting with Paley to discuss this important matter.

If I said yes, make the call, I was risking my relationship with Backe, but I felt the situation was too important. So a meeting was set with Paley, Backe, Leonard, and me. We met in my conference room, where I sat across from Paley and Leonard sat across from Backe.

Paley asked what this meeting was all about. I began by explaining the situation, the difficulty in replacing Cronkite, our choice of Rather, why him versus other alternatives, and the serious interest of ABC News. When I mentioned the money, Backe again stated his opposition to paying a CBS employee that much.

I then slipped Paley a piece of paper that said one rating point equaled $5 million! After a few seconds of silence, Paley said, "It has been my experience that what sometimes seems the most expensive investment turns out to be the cheapest."

With that statement, Leonard and I looked at each other and knew we had our deal—meeting over! Backe was not happy but accepted the decision. After the meeting, Leonard called Leibner and said the deal was done: $8 million over five years.

It wasn't long after that *Time* magazine put Rather's photo on the cover with the title *The Eight Million Dollar Man*. It was publicity we could have done without. Nevertheless, Rather fulfilled my prediction that the *CBS Evening News* would be number one, and he sat in the anchor chair for twenty-four years. That record will never be broken!

It was only after CBS lost major affiliated stations in large cities that the *CBS Evening News* fell into third place, from which it will never recover. The situation was further harmed when CBS management appointed Katie Couric as the anchor. The wrong person in the wrong position further drove audiences to the competition.

As for Dan Rather's tenure, he was everything we expected, and then some. He was worth everything CBS paid him. By to-day's standards, one could even argue he was *under*paid. If only the industry had more Dan Rathers today.

Roger Mudd was a very competent journalist and a good broadcaster, so when we selected Rather as the next anchor-man, I was hoping he would stay with CBS. His 1979 interview with Senator Edward Kennedy was outstanding. When he asked Kennedy why he wanted to be president, Kennedy stumbled for a response. It was so damaging that some believe the interview cost Kennedy the presidency.

The interview was pretaped, and the news team thought it might require an equal time response. We showed it to the corporate lawyers, and they recommended we not air it. But the story was too important, and not to broadcast it would be a journalistic error.

Airing it was a risk worth taking, so, against legal advice, it ran. Unfortunately, running the story did not help us keep Mudd at CBS. Disappointed at not being selected for the anchorman position, he left CBS to join NBC, where he stayed for a while before leaving to join PBS, after which he eventually retired.

∾

Another one of the great journalists of my era was Bill Moyers, a top-notch reporter and a great analyst. He was being sought after by ABC and NBC, and I wanted him to stay a key part of CBS News.

After being wooed by the competition, Moyers decided to make his home at CBS. Upon his decision, he sent me this letter:

Dear Gene,

I called yesterday to say, "You've done it, for better or for worse." The emphasis is decidedly on you because you made this happen. I've watched what you've done to support and expand news at CBS, and I listened to you talk about the future, and I'm convinced you meant it.

My discussions with Roone Arledge last year and my knowledge of Thorton Bradshaw, an old friend, leave no doubt that the competition is going to be fierce.

Roone intends to be first. I believe you want CBS to be first and best. And that excites me. When I arrive, it will be enthusiastically to do my best to justify your faith and expectations.

Thanks for the patience and persistence.

Bill

Moyers stayed at CBS and delivered everything expected of him. He provided analysis during election coverage and contributed thought-provoking commentary on the *CBS Evening News*. Unfortunately for CBS and for Moyers, CBS News could not provide enough airtime for long-form documentaries, which were his forte. Sadly for CBS, Moyers left the network in 1986 to join PBS, where he was able to fulfill his program aspirations on a broader scale. His work in public broadcasting justified my belief in his great talent as a journalist. He continued his outstanding work at PBS and then at NBC and MSNBC. His overall record in television demonstrated that Bill Moyers was one of the best journalists of his era.

∾

Public Relations: How to Turn a Problem into a Positive Event

One morning in 1981, no sooner had I walked into my office when Judy Stabile, my outstanding assistant, said I had a telephone call from the publisher of the *Buffalo News*. I sensed a problem brewing. When I returned his call, he told me that Morley Safer had made comments on a national broadcast about the city of Buffalo that he felt were insulting to the city and its residents.

What was it exactly that Morley said that was so improper? It seems that Safer gave a report about Chinese chefs who traveled to Buffalo to learn American-style cooking. At the conclusion of his report, he made the comment, "I guess they want to learn about boiling hot dogs." The comment so riled some of the citizens that they wanted an apology from Safer and CBS News.

I said I would look into it. So I called Safer. He had chosen the story obviously for humor, and had not intended it to be a malicious report. So I suggested we try to turn the event into a positive piece of publicity for Safer and CBS.

I scheduled a meeting with the mayor of Buffalo and the chief executive of Erie County. We flew to Buffalo with our wives for lunch and a series of meetings with city leaders and a tour of new developments throughout the city. The event generated a lot of publicity with newspaper and television coverage of Morley speaking and apologizing for his remarks. As a result, he was given both a key to the city and to Erie County on "Morley Safer Day."

The conclusion of the day included dinner at the Buffalo Hilton, where the Chinese chefs trained. It was delicious. The highlight was an opening course of large boiled peanuts we were required to eat with chopsticks. They were as tender as mashed potatoes!

The entire trip was a good example of how to turn "lemons into lemonade."

∽

Indeed, as president of the CBS Broadcast Group, every morning when I arrived at my office, I never knew what new situations I would face that day. It could be a telephone call from the publisher of the *Buffalo News,* a report from an unhappy viewer, or a question from one of my executives about a situation that needed a resolution.

Perhaps the most painful morning of my tenure was on April 13, 1982, when I arrived at my office and was informed about the slaying of three CBS employees the previous evening. Three CBS technicians leaving work at the CBS Broadcast Center on West 57th Street were shot as they went to their cars on the roof of Pier 92 nearby, which extended into the Hudson River.

They stumbled upon the abduction of a woman on the rooftop parking lot by a man with a van. Seeing that she was in peril, the men tried to intervene, then fled as he presented a gun. All three were shot by the assailant, who then sped away with the woman. She was abducted and slain in the van. It was revealed later that the woman was one of two witnesses in a federal fraud investigation. The defendant had hired a hitman to kill them, which he did. Both defendant and assassin ultimately were convicted and sentenced to jail time.

I felt I owed it to the CBS employees' families to offer condolences on behalf of CBS. I did not know the men, but as president of the group, I felt I had to personally visit the families and share my feelings of grief and sorrow. I tried to imagine the shock and emotional pain the families had to feel after sending their husbands off to work, only to find later that they would not be coming home, having been murdered trying to save a woman's life. These were the saddest and most difficult conversations I had with anyone, at any time, during my tenure as president.

∽

48 Hours

The news program *48 Hours* premiered in 1986. The original broadcast was titled *48 Hours on Crack Street,* a documentary for which a team of news correspondents followed drug users, police enforcement over the course of forty-eight hours to investigate and record the drug activity plaguing the cities, towns, and suburbs of America.

The program eventually evolved into *48 Hours,* a news

magazine that investigates crime and justice issues that affect many dimensions of the human experience.

During the years it has been broadcast, the program has received multiple Emmy, Peabody, and Edward R. Murrow awards. The fact that the program still maintains its popularity is a tribute to the many talented people who are a part of the broadcast. The producers, directors, and correspondents responsible for each program are dedicated professionals committed to putting a factual television show on the air. The quality of their work is self-evident, and the success of the program is further ratified by its enduring popularity in the television syndication market.

CBS Sports

NFL Football

I officially became president and chief executive officer of the CBS Broadcast Group in October 1977. I barely had a chance to warm my office seat when Pete Rozelle, Commissioner of the National Football League, called. The NFL's four-year football contract with CBS was expiring, and it was time to consider the new four-year deal.

But, as I learned, one really did not negotiate a contract with the NFL. Rozelle simply stated, "This is the number we expect each year for the next four years." For each year of the new contract, Rozelle wanted $44 million. Considering that CBS had been paying $22 million a year for the previous contract, the new number was quite a jolt! Was it possible for CBS to generate enough revenue with the new contract? How? What if we did not reach an agreement with the NFL, and the network had to find other programs to fill the hours on a Sunday afternoon? What would be the cost of substitute programming, and what revenues might that programming generate? What about the impact on affiliated stations when they no longer had football games in their cities?

Clearly, the National Football League is a powerful force in the country, not just as a formidable source of entertainment, but also as an economic powerhouse that generates millions of dollars for TV stations and their communities. It is a known fact that cities have agreed to owners' demands for new stadiums rather than risk the financial impact of losing a team to another city.

After serious consideration of all of these factors, and realizing that Rozelle had close relationships with some of the advertisers and was certain to have done his analysis of what the market would be willing to pay, we renewed the rights to broadcast the games for $44 million a year. Two other factors went into our decision. When negotiating for a prime-time schedule of ads, it was always helpful if the schedule could include a commercial in high-rated football games, even though those non-football dollars are not included in a profit and loss statement for the NFL agreement. Also, it is more valuable to put a promotional announcement for an upcoming entertainment program in a high-rated football game than in a show that may only have an audience of 10 percent in size. In effect, football on a Sunday afternoon can affect the ratings performance of entertainment shows anytime in the week. And by the end of the new contract, the NFL games were profitable for CBS.

During the four years the contract was in effect, I had an opportunity to become friendly with Rozelle and his close advisors, including some of the team owners, like Art Modell of the Cleveland Browns and Gene Klein of the San Diego Chargers, who were both on the NFL's television broadcast committee. The mutual respect we had came into play in 1982 when CBS was presented with the next new agreement to secure the broadcast rights to the NFC. The NFL asked for $150 million dollars a year for five years! This was more than three times larger per year than the previous agreement. That request was a real shocker!

I called Rozelle and told him there was no way CBS could afford the new deal. I had a sense that Rozelle was somewhat sympathetic to my plight. He said the number had come from the TV committee, and it would be best if I talked directly with one of the members. I was in California and made arrangements to meet with Gene Klein in Palm Springs, where he owned a home. Klein, a successful car dealer, was disappointed when I said CBS would not carry the games at that high a fee. But he said if CBS did not renew, they would take the games to the independent stations. I knew this was not practical for the NFL and would have repercussions with the other team owners.

Here is an excerpt from Klein's 1987 book, *First Down and a Billion*, describing our meeting:

Negotiations remained stalled. Then one day Gene Jankowski, President of CBS, called and asked if we might discuss the problem personally. I invited him out to my home in Palm Springs. When he arrived, we sat by the pool, watching golfers stroll by on the nearby course, and casually chatted about several hundred million dollars. His people had examined and reexamined the figures, Gene explained, and there was just no way CBS could pay what we were asking. Gene Jankowski is a very astute businessman and an excellent negotiator. But I must admit I wasn't moved to tears of sympathy for the network.

I had also looked at the figures. My bottom line added up differently from his bottom line. So, when he finished explaining his position, I asked, "Does this mean you don't want to televise the NFL?"

"That's not what I said, Gene. Of course we do."

"Well then," I told him, "this is what it's going to

cost you. We can sit here for a day, a week, or a month, but these are the numbers. This is equivalent to what the other shops are paying. You either take it or you don't." I was very firm; I did not give him the impression that those numbers were negotiable. That's where being secure, confident, even arrogant, comes in. Of course, Jankowski gave me the firm impression that CBS would not possibly accept those numbers. He too was secure, confident, even arrogant. That's what made negotiating with him so much fun for me. I'm not sure how he felt about it.

Our meeting was cordial, but finally Jankowski sighed and said, "I can't believe this, but I really don't think we're going to be able to make a deal."

Oh, the old sigh-and-walk-away ploy. "Well, I think you know I'm sorry about that. I want you to know that I have the utmost respect for CBS and for you, and this doesn't make me any happier than it does you, believe me. But I'm sure the network'll survive without the NFL, and I know the NFL'll survive without CBS."

"What are you going to do?"

It was kind of him to be concerned about our welfare. "Oh, don't worry about that," I reassured him, "we'll figure out something. I wish we could have gotten together, but I appreciate your position and I hope you understand mine. If the numbers don't add up for you, there's nothing you can do. Personally, I think you're doing the right thing if that's the case."

He left without making a proposal, but at least we were dancing . . . .

Pete Rozelle called a few days later with Jankowski's new offer. It was in the ballpark, still in the bleachers, but in the ballpark. We came down a bit, they came up a little, we came down a little more, they came up a little less, but eventually we reached an agreement.[1]

Eventually, CBS received a $50 million reduction in the rights fee. Fortunately, as a result of our agreement, CBS was the only network to make a profit at the end of the contract period.

During my time as president of CBS Broadcasting, I had three negotiations with Rozelle for rights to cover the NFL games. Because of the importance of the games to CBS, I used any opportunity I had to develop a personal relationship with Pete and Carrie Rozelle. The mutual respect we had came into play during the difficult discussion with Gene Klein during our second renewal, as described above.

Eventually, when Rozelle retired from the NFL commissioner position and moved to San Diego, I presented him with a special pair of CBS cufflinks as a sign of our appreciation and respect.

This was part of his letter in response:

Dear Gene,
It was good to get together with you and have a simple one-on-one lunch and get the update on your fascinating new business. The extra special CBS "eye" cuff links are really wonderful, and I can hardly wait to show Carrie. Also, they should last a long time because of my new West Coast informal wardrobe.

Best wishes, my friend, as you like Carrie and myself, enter an exciting new phase in our lives.

Regards,
Pete

---

1. Klein, Gene, and David Fisher, *First Down and a Billion: The Funny Business of Pro Football* (New York: William Morrow & Company Inc, 1987), 111-112.

Rozelle was NFL commissioner for almost thirty years. The outstanding growth and popularity of professional football is due in large measure to his leadership—a great legacy!

∽

The Masters Golf Tournament

As president of CBS Broadcasting, I had the privilege to attend all of the prestigious sporting events covered by our sports division. This included National Football League games, the Super Bowl, "March Madness," the NCAA basketball championship, the Kentucky Derby and Belmont Stakes horse races, and various golf tournaments.

By far, the most impressive event I attended was The Masters Tournament, a professional golf tournament held every year since 1934, at Augusta National Golf Club in Augusta, Georgia, in early April. In the simplest terms, the tournament is just another four days of golf on the professional tour. However, the leadership of the Masters has set very high standards for all those involved: the golfers, the patrons (attendees are not referred to as fans, as at other tournaments), and the network personnel working on the broadcast.

The patrons have standards they are expected to follow in terms of behavior, including choice of food, how they dispose of waste, and how they shop for Masters memorabilia. The caddies, too, are subject to standards, beginning with the all-white jumpsuits they must wear during the rounds of golf.

CBS began broadcasting the Masters in 1956. Every year since, the contract with Augusta has been for one year; renewal is subject to how satisfied the Masters leadership is with CBS's coverage of the previous tournament. CBS technicians have buried over thirty miles of television cables at Augusta in order to provide maximum flexibility in covering the eighteen holes and surrounding venues.

Advertisers are also subject to high standards. Masters management decides which sponsors they want, how much they pay, and how many commercial announcements are made during the games. After each broadcast, a meeting would be held between tournament executives and CBS production people to review the highs and lows of the day's coverage. More than once, CBS was asked to remove an on-air commentator for comments deemed to be improper for the image of the Masters. In 1994, commentator Gary McCord joked that the fast-putting greens must not have been mowed but bikini waxed. Goodbye, Mr. McCord!

I use the Masters tournament as an example of what businesses can do to stand apart from their competitors. Set high standards. Insist on quality execution. Insist on maintaining close relations with clients. Do not tolerate lax employee performance. Develop a robust and recognizable appearance in internal and external communications. At CBS, we had what was called a "secretarial booklet" that outlined the standardized preparation of correspondence. All CBS stationery used the same typeface, and letter paper had a very faint dot of where the first letter should be placed in the salutation.

Ludwig Mies van der Rohe, the famous architect, coined the phrase, "God is in the details." He meant that whatever one does should be done thoroughly. Even minor details are important. The Masters is a classic example of caring about the details.

During one Masters tournament, I walked the course to say hello to a cameraman on the seventeenth fairway. He invited me over the restraining rope to show me how difficult it was to cover the ball coming off the tee and follow it down the fairway. The next day, I received a call from Hord Hardin, the Masters chairman. When I went to his office, he complained to me that someone was talking to a cameraman, which was forbidden. I did not know if he knew it was me, but he wanted to spread the word that no one should do that again. How he found out about the perceived offense, I had no idea. But it illustrates how much attention the tournament management pays to the little details that affect their standards.

For four days in April, the Masters golf tournament is the epitome of how attention to details results in quality leadership and an impressive image. When evaluating the Masters, or for that matter, any company business, the first items to examine are the assets of the corporation. There are the traditional assets, the ones on balance sheets that have a specific value in the marketplace. In a sense, these kinds of assets could be called commonplace: the fact that they have an agreed upon value means that there is no mystery about them.

However, there is another category of assets whose worth is much harder to assess. And yet, they may provide the critical margin that separates success from failure, leadership from mediocrity, and purpose from drift. These sorts of assets are more likely to be qualities than quantities, concepts like character and tradition and the conditions that flow from them. Insiders can feel them and outsiders can sense them, but they cannot be lined up and put on display. Nevertheless, they are a powerful, active ingredient in the success of an organization.

When these assets are present, they enhance other strengths. They influence the style and sensitivity with which even ordinary things are done. They have to do with both dignity and decency, and they are the wellspring for the kind of pride that transcends quantifiable achievements. They can cause certain actions to be taken and others to be avoided. They are most evident in moments of trial, when they provide a critical edge of energy and will. And yet, they are quietly part of the most routine of tasks. To have them is to have a kind of secret weapon, one that is especially valuable because its formula cannot be stolen and its design cannot be duplicated.

It may be more significant to have this extra tier of assets in broadcasting than in many other businesses for two reasons. The first is that all broadcasters bring the same potential to the table and play according to the same rules. Therefore, differentiation must be created. When it is, its effects are multiplied. Secondly, broadcasters don't have a physical product in the usual sense of the term. They don't grow things, or extricate them from the ground, or have machines to manufacture them. What broadcasters make cannot be worn, or weighed, or touched in the usual sense. Their product is generated by one set of people and its success depends on another set of people deciding to accept or reject it. It has no other existence. Since what they do comes entirely out of people's minds, it is obvious that the state of those minds is of the greatest importance. In fact, I believe that a long record of leadership cannot be explained except through the presence of these hidden assets.

I believe that the history of CBS News was a case in point. From the moment of its formation, in the quality of its staff, and in the standards they set, CBS News always had that indefinable extra dimension that fascinated audiences and frustrated competitors.

Sadly, later in my career at CBS I witnessed changes in management and mergers of the company with other entities that caused the loss of many, if not all, of its valuable, intangible traditions of quality, and as a result, CBS's prized reputation as the "Tiffany network."

∾

The Olympics

During my tenure as president, I was involved with the negotiations for two Olympics: the 1984 Winter Olympics in Sarajevo and the 1988 Summer Olympics in Seoul. Although CBS did not obtain the broadcast rights for either event, both experiences were very educational.

CBS was invited to compete for the Sarajevo coverage in 1979. To compete effectively, we had to go to Yugoslavia and spend time with the country's organizing committee. So a group of us flew on the CBS company plane to Sarajevo, with a refueling stop in Shannon, Ireland.

When we arrived at our final destination, the first thing I noticed was the smell in the air. It was evident that the city used a lot of fossil fuel! I guessed it was coal.

The negotiating committee made clear to us that the reason Yugoslavia wanted the Olympics was to show the world that the country was capable of being a more important player on the world stage. A great deal of work would have to be done to prepare the city and facilities for the beginning of the Games.

While in Sarajevo, I had an opportunity to do some sightseeing. The city is the site of the assassination of Archduke Franz Ferdinand of Austria and his wife in 1914, acknowledged to be a catalyst for the outbreak of World War I. There are footprints in cement on the sidewalk where Gavrilo Princip stood when he fired the pistol that killed the two members of the Habsburg Empire. The street where it occurred was about two car lanes wide. Shooting two people in an open automobile that for some reason had stopped would not be a difficult feat.

CBS's bid of $90 million was outdone by ABC's bid of $95 million. Strangely, Roone Arledge, president of ABC Sports, never made the trip to the city. I often wondered why! Sadly, all of the Olympic committee's effort and hard work was forgotten by 1992, with the outbreak of the Bosnian War.

∾

In 1982, CBS was invited to go to South Korea and compete for the rights to broadcast the 1988 Summer Olympics. James Rosenfield, president of the network, and Neal Pilson, head of CBS Sports, and I were the negotiating committee. We flew to Korea on separate flights; I flew on Korean Air Lines 007, a large 747 airplane that took me from New York City to Anchorage, Alaska, for a quick stop, then on to Seoul. The following year, a Korean Air 007 flight was shot down by a Soviet fighter aircraft, and over two hundred people perished. Within a week, the Soviet Union went from denying they were responsible to holding a press conference to explain how and why it happened. I felt that for the first time, the Soviets were now in the public relations business!

Once our team settled in Seoul, we agreed that we would all go to a Korean tailor known for making good suits for low prices, with very fast service. The tailor lived up to his reputation. We each bought a three-piece suit. We were fitted on Wednesday and had the finished suits by Friday. What we did not focus on was that we had all selected the same blue pinstripe fabric. One evening, when the American ambassador to Korea, Richard Walker, hosted a cocktail reception for us and our Korean hosts at the embassy, the three of us wore our new suits. In the reception line, we looked like formal members of the embassy staff!

I was very impressed with the Korean executives and politicians that we met. Many of them had PhDs from American universities, including my alma mater, Michigan State. They were smart and personable. We were made to feel amazingly comfortable.

As part of our visit, the Olympic committee insisted we visit the 38th parallel, the dividing line between North and South Korea. So we went to Panmunjom, a memorable experience! On the drive back to Seoul, I noticed immense concrete blocks suspended above the roadway. "What are those?" I asked.

"In the event the North invaded the South, the blocks would be dropped on the road to make it more difficult for invaders to move swiftly," was the response.

How sad it is to see a nation of people divided by political beliefs.

At the end of our visit, we agreed to further meetings in California before submitting our final offer. Once again, after analyzing the event, the logistics of games in another time zone and how that could affect revenue potential, our final bid was not the highest.

While I was a bit disappointed in not securing the rights to the Olympic Games, I took comfort in knowing that the strength of the network is in its weekly news, entertainment, and sports programs with an emphasis on ongoing events—i.e., basketball, football, and golf. The consistent strength of CBS Sports is more valuable than the occasional high-profile event that may or may not be profitable.

∞

Baseball

One major contract that CBS Sports did not have was Major League Baseball. Each fall, the World Series would impact our prime-time schedule, so in 1984 I went to see MLB commissioner

Bowie Kuhn. The games were shared between NBC and ABC, with each network paying $500 million for the rights for four years. I suggested the league should have three packages, one for each network, similar to the National Football League. Kuhn said he hoped to do that at some time, but not during the next few years. ABC and NBC renewed their contracts for four more years, but after ABC was into the deal for a year and a half, Capital Cities Broadcasting acquired the network. They did not like the numbers relating to baseball.

One day, my phone rang. It was Peter Ueberroth, the new baseball commissioner, who said he wanted to see me. At a meeting in my office, Ueberroth said ABC was willing to pay $50 million to have CBS take over the remaining two years of their contract! We did our homework and decided the money generated by two and a half years of sales, plus the $50 million from ABC, would not be profitable. We passed. Many years later, CBS would not make as smart a decision.

Weston, Connecticut,
and an Unwelcome Visitor

W e purchased our house in Weston in 1980, because we outgrew the Westport home and simply needed more space for our growing family. Our children Carole and Peter had been joined by daughters Judith in 1965 and Jennifer in 1967.

Weston had no sewers or commercial water system, so most of the town had to rely on septic systems and deep-water wells. Most of the property to protect this environmental need was zoned for two acres. Larger properties were not uncommon.

Because of its location, architecture, layout, and comfort, at the time, I referred to 83 Kettle Creek Road as our "forever house." However, one of its shortcomings was the fact that the basement had no external door. Anything we wanted to put in the basement for storage, my workshop, children's playthings, etc., had to be brought through the house and through the center hall door and down the stairs.

Imagine, then, the reaction I had one evening when Peter rushed up to me when I arrived home from my New York City commute and in a very excited fashion informed me that we had a skunk in our basement. A real live skunk! I did not believe him. For a skunk—or anyone else—to get to our basement, they had to walk into the house, pass through the kitchen, or, if they chose, the front door, go from the hall, turn right into the center hall, open the door, and descend the stairs. There were no open windows. No holes in the wall. Nothing but solid cement!

A live skunk? In our basement? No way!

But our son was very smart. And very observant. Better to err on the side of the wise, etc. So we went to the hall door. Gently, very gently, we opened the door. Quietly, very quietly we descended the stairs.

And there it was! A puff of black and white under a corner of my work bench. Now what? Is there a boy or man alive who has not sniffed, smelled, or been overwhelmed by the foulest fragrance of a scared skunk?

My emotions were mixed. My questions many. How did this happen? How did it get there? How do we get it out? How do we get it out without spraying? What if it sprays? How do we get rid of the smell? Do we ever get rid of the smell?

And what if all the answers to these questions are—you don't? You don't get it out. You don't get it out without spraying. You don't get rid of the smell. You don't ever get rid of the smell.

So there we sat at 7 p.m. on a midweek evening, trying to solve a problem we were sure that no one had ever faced in recorded history! How to get rid of an uninvited skunk in the basement of an elegantly decorated Early American home without creating a stench guaranteed to permeate the walls, wallpaper, fabric, furniture, bedrooms, kitchen, carpets, family room, dining room, kitchen, and possibly become immortalized in the framework so that our house would be forever known as the Skunk House!

So what did we do? We did what any self-respecting homeowner would do under similar conditions. We called the SPCA.

Me: Hello, SPCA. I'm yada, yada. I have a skunk in the basement. Can you help me?

SPCA: Yes sir, no problem. We will send two men with a tarpaulin. They walk down the stairs and throw the tarp over the skunk. They wrap it up and take it away.

Me: And it doesn't spray?

SPCA: Oh sir, we don't guarantee that it won't spray, but if it does, that is your problem.

Me: That doesn't make good sense to me. It is too risky. Tell me about skunks.

SPCA: They love chicken. They dislike the smell of ammonia.

Me: Thank you very much. We will call you if we need you.

Fortunately, we had leftover cold chicken in the refrigerator. And our laundry room had its requisite supply of household ammonia.

Nevertheless, Peter and I had to determine how the skunk had managed to enter our basement without having to open the center hall door!

Upon investigation we discovered a very small triangular opening beneath the back hall stairs leading from our garage. The garage door had been left open as a welcome invitation to the creatures of the night and our young skunk accepted the opportunity.

His adventure was complicated by the fact that once he went through the triangle, his trip was met with a shocking development as he fell off a four-foot wall into the basement. Wonder of wonders, he did not let go of his weapon.

Armed with the knowledge provided by the SPCA, we found a ten-foot board, six inches wide, in our yard. This was the ramp that hopefully would provide our unwanted stranger a graceful way to climb out of our cherished basement and eventually return to his proper element.

To offer encouragement, we poured ample amounts of

ammonia onto paper towels and tossed them in such a manner as to build a barrier to prevent further exploration of our basement.

Next, we took the cooked chicken, broke it into pieces, and placed them about ten inches apart on the inclined plank. In Hansel and Gretel style, we hoped to lead our unwanted guest on a more painless way out of our nether regions.

Then we placed a laundry shirt cardboard tent by the hole where he entered. With one last flourishing toss of an ammonia-filled towel toward his resting spot, we closed the basement door and went to bed.

The following morning, we reversed the process.

We checked the tent in the garage. It was tipped over.

We carefully opened the basement door and checked the inclined plank. The chicken was gone.

We looked under the workbench. The skunk was gone!

Voila! No skunk. And no smell!

And eureka, newfound knowledge about skunks, the SPCA, power of ammonia, appetite appeal of cold chicken, and another use for shirt cardboards.

∽

My weekends and summers were mainly occupied with a wide range of family activities: Little League baseball games, field hockey, tennis, gardening, visits to the zoo and Beardsley Park, swimming at Compo Beach in Westport, skiing in Vermont, sailing to Nantucket, and vacations in Boothbay Harbor, Maine, and a train trip to Disney World in Florida.

The return trip from Florida via Amtrak was unforgettable. En route home, our Amtrak train collided with a freight train, and three of the cars were knocked off the rails. Sally and I were sitting in the club car when we felt the impact—so our first thoughts were of the children's safety. However, we were soon reunited and all were okay. The passengers had to disembark and await US Marine Corps buses that took everyone to Union Station in Washington, DC. Our luggage was still on the train, so Peter and I went back into the train car and retrieved our bags. As the car was leaning sideways and in danger of flipping, we did so very gently! From DC, we caught a train to Westport and arrived home tired but safe.

While I may not have spent as much time with my children as some other parents did with theirs, I tried to make up for any shortfall by taking them to special events with me, so they had stories to tell their friends. Thus, my kids went to Super Bowls, Final Four basketball games, US Open tennis, and the Masters golf. I was sorry to see my children grow up so fast. One day they are in grammar school, and soon they are off to college!

Notable Newsmakers

Donald Trump

I t was a beautiful early autumn day in the early 1980s. The sky was a bright blue, the temperature was mild, and the air was fresh and invigorating: a perfect day to take a boat ride on the Hudson River. That is what Sally and I were going to do on that fall day. Peter Dawkins, who won the Heisman as an an all-American halfback for the Army Cadet football team at the United States Military Academy at West Point, had invited us as his guest to take a boat from the west side of Manhattan to the dock at West Point. Other guests included Peter Cohen, CEO at the investment firm Shearson Lehman Brothers; Dan Sargent, an executive at Salomon Brothers, and his wife Elaine (they were friends of Sally's and mine); Ivana and Donald Trump; and Judy, Peter's wife.

Dawkins is a remarkable individual. Not only was he an All American football player, but he was also head of his class, a Rhodes Scholar, and an all-star rugby player while pursuing his studies in England. He retired from the Army after twenty-four years with the rank of brigadier general in 1983, and went on to have an extremely successful career as a financial executive. When the boat arrived at West Point, Dawkins had arranged for us to be met by a bus with his name across the front. We were taken to the dining hall where we had a delicious meal, after which we watched the cadet corps lead everyone into Michie Stadium: very impressive and very emotional! After the game, we boarded the bus to the boat and enjoyed the ride back to Manhattan.

It was during the hours of that afternoon that I had my first conversations with Ivana and Donald Trump. Ivana told me about growing up in Czechoslovakia, and about how much she enjoyed skiing and was good enough to make the Olympics. Donald and I talked briefly about broadcasting and little else.

Months later, he called me and invited me to lunch at the "21" Club on West 52nd Street. We met on the second floor of the iconic restaurant, at which time he made his request. The Trump organization owned a lot of real estate north of Manhattan, which included railroad facilities. He asked me if I would consider moving the CBS Broadcast Center from West 57th Street to his land north of the Harlem River.

My response was immediate: "Sorry, but no."

Trump was unhappy with my quick decision, but I saw no need to spend time studying his proposal. It would make no sense to move our entire television production facilities out of Manhattan to a location that would increase the cost of operations, cause more travel time for our talent, and lead to other inefficiencies only discovered should the move take place.

The next time I saw Trump was in the same dining room at "21," when I was having lunch with a client and he was across the room having lunch with Marla Maples, whom he eventually married after leaving Ivana. I never would have believed that he would become the President of the United States. Even if I did, I still would not have moved the broadcast center to his railroad yard!

∾

Speaking of future presidents, while I was at CBS, I was fortunate enough to meet Presidents Jimmy Carter, Ronald Rea-
gan, and George H.W. Bush while they were in office and Bill
Clinton when he was governor of Arkansas. I also met international figures like Pope John Paul II (and later Pope Francis),
and the "Queen Mum," Queen Elizabeth the Queen Mother.
Through CBS and my affiliation with the AFI, I also met many
of the members of Hollywood royalty, including Gregory Peck,
Jimmy Stewart, and Tony Curtis. Many of the high-profile politicians, athletes, celebrities, and artists I encountered remained
acquaintances, but many also became friends. At times, my personal and professional life wove seamlessly together, making
for a lifetime of remarkable experiences.

∾

Martha Stewart

I first met Martha in 1986 at a dinner party hosted by Richard
Brandt at his home in Westport, Connecticut. Richard was a
neighbor of Martha and her husband, Andrew. Richard was the
chairman of the Trans-Lux Corporation and chairman of the
American Film Institute, of which I was also a board member.

Andrew Stewart was in book publishing and saw the potential of creating books around his wife's skills as a caterer, enter-
tainer, and home and garden designer. His instincts were correct.
A series of books by Martha Stewart were successful and laid the
foundation for what eventually became a Stewart empire.

A few years later, Brandt hosted a fun lunch at his home

dedicated to getting physically fit. It included a healthful meal, a lecture, and exercises. Martha was there, and participated enthusiastically in the program. It was while we were taking a short rest that she told me how hurt she was when her husband took up with a young woman at his office, a painful occurrence that ended the marriage in 1990.

Over the next few years, Martha had social functions at Turkey Hill, her four-acre estate in Westport, where she raised vegetables and flowers. She also had a barn on the property that was used for photography for her books and as a set for her television appearances. One morning at 7 a.m. my phone rang. It was Martha, inviting Sally and me to a party that night at her farm. The party was photographed, and the photos appeared in *Martha Stewart's Christmas: Entertaining, Decorating, Giving,* published in 1989.

In 1991, when I was chairman of the board of the American Film Institute, I had a holiday party at my apartment on Fifth Avenue in New York City. I invited Martha, and she arrived with four compact discs she had produced to provide music while entertaining—another new idea! The party was a success, and guests included Cicely Tyson, the award-winning actress; Dan Rather; John Mack of Morgan Stanley; Don Burke, president of ABC; and other fans of the movies.

While I was living in Weston, my mother-in-law, who lived with us, would visit the senior citizens' social club. While there, she met and became friendly with Martha Kostyra, Martha Stewart's mother. On the few occasions I saw Martha senior, I was impressed with her vitality and warmth. I could understand where Martha Stewart obtained her energy and talent.

∽

Our apartment on 67th and Fifth Avenue, which we purchased around 1985, was the site of too many memorable occasions to count. It had a great wraparound terrace, from which I could have washed all the windows from the outside—if I'd wanted to! I'd stay in the city one or two nights a week, and Sally and I would often come in on the weekends as well.

The apartment was the site of an unforgettable twentieth anniversary party for *60 Minutes* in 1988. Everyone was there: Don Hewitt, Mike Wallace, Harry Reasoner, Meredith Viera, Andy Rooney, and more. Viera brought her two-year-old son, Ben. I had an upright Baldwin piano, and little Ben started banging on the keys, which greatly upset Hewitt. The dinner was a buffet, with everyone finding a place to sit around the apartment. Bill Paley, Andy Rooney, and I ended up sitting around a desk. Paley was telling stories, and Andy Rooney was listening and eating away. Dessert was served, and I brought three strawberry tarts back to our places. As Paley was still talking and talking, I watched as Andy Rooney reached over with his fork and took a big scoop out of Paley's strawberry tart.

The look on Paley's face! He looked at me and then looked at Andy. "Whatcha doing? You're eating my dessert!" Andy just laughed. I wish I had that on tape.

Andy Rooney was quite a character. He was self-assured, and didn't care about anything. He was very successful as part of the *60 Minutes* team—but he also figured that if CBS ever fired him, he still had his popular newspaper syndicated column. So he did what he wanted. He and I had a nice relationship.

In the 1990s, Sally and I hosted a dinner at our house in Fairfield, Connecticut. It was quite a table: Jack Paar, the former host of NBC's *The Tonight Show*, and his wife, Miriam; Andy Rooney and his wife, Margie; the actor James Naughton and his wife, Pamela; and Pat Collins, the TV critic, and her husband Bill Sarnoff, the chairman of Warner Books. Naughton and I were at one end of the table, Paar was sitting at the other with Rooney on one side, and Sally on the other. Paar and Rooney were reminiscing about the Second World War, the *Stars and Stripes*, and stories from the military. Naughton started talking to me. Paar stopped and bellowed to Naughton, "Why are *you* talking when *I'm* talking at this end of the table?" Every time I would see Naughton, he'd bring it up, and we'd have a good laugh.

LA Stories

I n 1977, entertainment decisions were primarily made in CBS's New York City headquarters. But we began to feel that just as one wouldn't have a sales staff in York, Pennsylvania, if all the ad agencies were on Madison Avenue, the same theory applied to our Entertainment division. Since so many of the creative ideas and the studios were in Hollywood, we posited that it would make more sense to transfer our Entertainment division to Los Angeles. So we transferred about 200 people out to Television City in California, and it helped CBS's performance immediately.

Working with the Entertainment division in Los Angeles gave me an opportunity to meet many studio executives, as well as many of the creators. I had dinner with Norman Lear numerous times. He was the creator of *All in the Family, One Day at a Time,* and a number of other successful programs on CBS. I came to know Lee Rich, co-founder and president of Lorimar Television, which produced the TV series *Knots Landing, Dallas, Falcon Crest,* and other big hits. (*The Waltons* was Lorimar's first claim to fame.)

It seemed that, not so long before, I had been a young kid wanting to get into broadcasting, and now I was the president of

CBS Broadcasting. Ultimately, I think that I had the best job in broadcasting that existed in the country. And as someone who had also played baseball quite seriously growing up, I dreamt of playing center field or pitching for the New York Yankees. Now, I felt in a sense that's exactly what I was doing, though as the head of the Broadcast Group.

∾

I built up some good relationships and even friendships with the people in the Entertainment division and in Hollywood. One of the talent agents I got to know in Los Angeles was Ed Hookstratten. He represented Phyllis George, who was on CBS, as well as Tom Brokaw and Tom Snyder on NBC, and a host of other actors and newscasters. He also had a relationship with the Los Angeles Dodgers and the Los Angeles Rams.

Ed went to the University of Southern California on a baseball scholarship as a left-handed pitcher. One night, we were having dinner at Chasen's, and the conversation turned to our experiences as college players. He said he wanted to see how good I was, and that the next time I came to Los Angeles, he would make arrangements for me to pitch in Dodger Stadium. I was not sure whether he was bluffing or just teasing me.

Nevertheless, in 1986 on my next trip to LA, I called Ed and said I was prepared to go to the stadium. True to his word, he made arrangements for me to show up at Tommy Lasorda's office, the manager of the Dodgers.

A uniform was hanging on the back door of Lasorda's office. "It's for you," said Hookstratten. "We're on the field in fifteen minutes."

In short order, I was on the field playing catch when Ron Perranoski, a pitching coach, started playing *serious* catch with me, telling me I was on the mound in five minutes!

And I was. I threw nothing but fastballs to the players. (Pedro Guerrero hit one of my pitches out of the park.) After I performed respectably, Lasorda asked me to pitch high fastballs to Steve Sax. He wanted Sax to get down on the ball because he was hitting too many fly balls. He felt many of his hits could become singles if he kept the ball down.

It was a fun afternoon until I realized the local CBS station was taping me, intending to run a piece on the evening sports show. That bothered me. I did not want word to get back to CBS in New York that the president was playing games in Hollywood. I forbade the use of the tape, a decision I came to regret the more I thought about it.

Some weeks later, when the Dodgers came to play the New York Mets, I took my daughters Jennifer and Judy to Shea Stadium early so we could go down to the dugout and say hello to Lasorda. Gracious as he was, he called Steve Sax over to meet the girls and gave each of them an autographed baseball.

I had actually met Lasorda before, when he was a left-handed pitcher for the Montreal Royals and they came to Buffalo to play the Bisons of the International League. I was a high school student attending the game. (He didn't remember that meeting. I never held it against him.)

∽

I always enjoyed these business trips to the West Coast. I had the opportunity to meet and develop friendly relationships with some of the best performers on CBS television, who would share interesting stories about events in their careers.

At one dinner, actress Angela Lansbury, the star of the long-running hit series *Murder, She Wrote*, said the starring role as Jessica Fletcher gave her more notoriety than she ever had, despite her decades-long career in motion pictures. On one occasion, she was on tour in Kansas City and took some clothes to a local dry cleaner. The person there was so pleased to be able to serve "Mrs. Fletcher"!

Another memorable LA evening was spent at the home of actor Danny Kaye in 1985. His other guests included Itzhak Perlman, the renowned violinist, and Peter O'Malley, whose family owned the Brooklyn and Los Angeles Dodgers baseball teams. Kaye was a remarkable man. Not only was he an outstanding film and television star, but he was also a gourmet chef and a licensed jet pilot.

∽

NCCS Award

Some months after the dinner at Kaye's home, I was asked to receive the 1985 Humanitarian Award from the National Conference of Christians and Jews entertainment division. The NCCJ was formed in 1928 to facilitate cooperation between religions on civics and social justice issues, and to promote understanding and mutual respect through education and dialogue. I asked Kaye if he would introduce me at the dinner, as he had been the first recipient of the Humanitarian Award.

The event was held at the Century Plaza Hotel, with 2,000 guests in attendance. Entertainment was provided by Gladys Knight and the Pips, with additional comments by John Madden. Charles Osgood, the anchor of *CBS Sunday Morning*, gave opening remarks and served as MC. He introduced Kaye, who made some positive comments about me. But when I walked forward with my speech, he took it from my hands and said I should not use notes but speak from the heart.

His gesture got a big laugh from the crowd and caused a

moment of panic for me. When the noise subsided, he returned my speech. But he was right: A moment like that called for a more informal response, even though my formal remarks captured the spirit of the event's occasion.

This is the way *Variety*, the show business publication, described the event:

Gene Jankowski—NCCJ's '85 Humanitarian— Nice Guy, Too

If you're a top network exec and your affiliates board sends a telegram saying you're "the original Mr. Nice Guy whose sense of fair play is at a level we can only hope to approach," you've got to be wondering if the stations are gearing up to demand more compensation. If you were CBS Broadcast Group Prez Gene Jankowski, Wednesday night, apparently the affils had no other motive than to say congratulations on being awarded the 22nd annual Humanitarian Award for the National Conference of Christians and Jews entertainment division. Danny Kaye, first recipient of the kudos in 1963, made the presentation to Jankowski in front of a packed Century Plaza Hotel ballroom. Echoing affil sentiments, Kaye called the honoree "an honorable, hard-working, tough businessman, who is nice." For his part, Jankowski noted that America has come out of two great depressions, one economic, one moral. "Recovery from the former is complete," he said, "but while progress against the latter is 'heartening,' there is no room for complacency. The country as a whole," said the CBS exec, "has experienced a 'national awakening' against discrimination," and he recalled his own, when his basketball team was traveling in North Carolina (quite a few years back) and the only black member had to eat separately from the rest of the team. "Nowhere," he went on, "is the new era more evident than in the broadcast industry," citing *The Cosby Show* for presenting a black family as people and not caricatures, and national morning news anchors (i.e., Bryant Gumbel and other on-camera minorities). The evening had a decidedly lighter feel early on when CBS sportscaster John Madden was shown in a video making his selection for the All-Madden team. Besides such potential gridders as Tom Selleck (quarterback), CBS Entertainment Prez Bud Grant (lineman), and Dan Rather (wide receiver), he selected Jankowski (nose tackle) as captain. "Cause he can be anything he wants." Additionally, Madden pointed out that besides being such a great gridiron name, Jankowski would never fit on the back of a jersey. CBS News anchor Charles Osgood lent his talented poetry to the proceedings as emcee, comprising rhyme with reason. He subbed for m.c. Bob Newhart, who due to illness, had decided to limit his activity only to his tele series. Entertainment was well provided by Gladys Knight and the Pips (ably backed up by the Michael Paige Orchestra), who batted out such numbers as "The Heat is On" and "Midnight Train to Georgia." The Pips provided locomotive choreography, while Knight's pipes led a full head of steam. Highlight of their act was a "Princely" spoof, topping the Purple Pip (Merrell Knight) and the rock and roll number, "Jankowski is a Star." The bit was carried off so well, it could become a regular on the fund raiser circuit.

Obviously, the evening was an unforgettable event for me. Sadly, however, the need for an organization like the NCCJ still exists. Discrimination existed then, and even though progress has been made over the years, discrimination still exists in our society. The struggle toward mutual respect among people continues. Hatred accomplishes nothing and only results in pain and misery.

∽

A *M*A*S*H* Farewell and a Holiday Trip

One failed attempt to get to Los Angeles turned out to be a fortunate twist of fate, and illustrated, once again, the importance of corporate relationships. One of the most popular programs on CBS was the war comedy drama *M*A*S*H*. It was broadcast for eleven years, and when the final episode, "Goodbye, Farewell and Amen," aired in 1983, it set a record for audience size and share of the viewing public.

To celebrate the conclusion of production, a "wrap party" was scheduled for a Sunday evening at 20th Century Fox, where the show was produced. Not one to miss an important event, I made arrangements to fly out of JFK Airport on an early afternoon Pan Am flight that would arrive in Los Angeles in the afternoon, giving me ample time to freshen up at my hotel and go to the studio for the party.

I boarded the plane, and we left the gate on schedule. However, we did not take off! The plane taxied to a hangar, where we were required to wait until the problem, whatever it was, was resolved. No one seemed to know what the issue was. Were we waiting for a new flight crew? Was there a mechanical problem? Regardless of the cause of the delay, we were required to stay on the aircraft. I kept looking at my watch, realizing that if the plane did not leave soon, I ran the risk of arriving in LA too late to attend the party.

We remained on the ground for four hours, at which point I realized I was going to miss the function. By the time the plane landed, all I could do was go to my hotel and go to bed. Fortunately, I had scheduled a lunch date the next day with Lee Rich, whose Lorimar Television programs were crucial to CBS's ratings success. After lunch, I went back to my hotel, made some phone calls, and left for the airport to return to New York.

The next morning, I wrote a letter to Pan Am explaining how disappointed I was in the airline's treatment of me and the plane full of passengers, and that I might not fly Pan Am again. Apparently, it got the attention of Pan Am management. I received a telephone call from Jeff Krendler, an airline vice president, who said he wanted to see me.

When he arrived in my office, he offered me two first-class tickets to any place Pan Am flew. I accepted his offer and said I was planning a Christmas trip to Switzerland and was looking for a hotel. He suggested the Victoria Jungfrau Grand Hotel & Spa in Interlaken. Historically a summer-only hotel, that Christmas would be the first time it would be open for the winter.

That confirmed my trip! I made reservations for Sally, our four children, and my mother-in-law, who was living with us in Connecticut. I felt Pan Am did alright by me. I received two free tickets and bought five first-class tickets for my family. The trip was everything one could hope for at Christmas. We walked to the Jungfrau Railway that took us up Eiger Mountain, went to midnight mass at a small church that had lit candles on the trees behind the altar, and heard *"Silent Night"* sung in German, as it was first performed.

I'm not certain the trip would have happened if my plane had not been delayed on my way to the *M*A*S*H* farewell function—and Pan Am retained a loyal customer!

∾

In the mid 1980s, I was invited to speak at a Hollywood Radio and TV Society industry luncheon. I spoke with John Mitchell, the chair of the Hollywood Society, in advance of the event. In the course of our conversation, I told him my story about John Frankenheimer: that when I was a student at Michigan State, wondering what to do next, I had read about him in *Time* magazine and was inspired by his story. When I arrived at the luncheon, there was John Frankenheimer. Mitchell had invited him to come attend the lunch and sit next to me on the dais.

Frankenheimer and I were fast friends. He invited me out to his house in Malibu. I met his wife, an actress named Evans Evans. His hobby was building models, and he gave me a tour of his collection. He was a talented film and television director, and we forged a nice relationship. It was a wonderful full-circle moment, of which my life has had many.

Navigating
Corporate Waters

One of my perks as president of the CBS Broadcast Group was a chauffeured limousine at my disposal. It was considered a luxury, so I paid tax for the privilege, but convenience and time-saving efficiency made it well worth it. My driver was Frank Knapik, a retired police officer from Bridgeport, Connecticut. Not only was he an excellent driver, but he was legally armed, so I always felt a high degree of security when he was behind the wheel.

One evening, as we pulled into the driveway in Weston, the first thing we noticed was a state trooper's vehicle by the entrance way to our house. That made my heart rate jump. As I got out of the car nervously, a state trooper came out of the front door, raised his hand, and said everything was okay.

"No problem."

Very comforting, but why was he there?

Sally had received a phone call about thirty minutes before. When she answered the phone, a male voice said he knew I was on my way home and I was going to be shot on the Merritt Parkway. Fortunately, she did not panic. She put the phone down, dropped to the floor, and crawled into an office we had off the kitchen where we had a second phone line and called the state police. After some discussion, it was concluded that it was probably a prank call by some sick-minded high school student who was having some "fun." I never did find out if the police even located the perpetrator.

However, the incident was another reminder of the visibility of my position, and why I felt a degree of comfort with an ex-police officer as my driver. This was not the first time I had been threatened. A few years earlier, Sally and I had taken two friends to dinner in New York City. Our plan was to eat at the Ground Floor Restaurant in the CBS Building, then go to the CBS Broadcast Center on 57th Street, where they were taping an episode of *Kate and Allie*, a sitcom starring Susan Saint James and Jane Curtin. When we finished dinner, a man from CBS security came up to me to say he had received a phone call that said if I showed up at the Broadcast Center, I would be shot. A sobering statement, to say the least.

What to do? Take it seriously and stay away? Consider it a prank call and go to the taping? So, I took it seriously, but risked that it was a prank, and felt I had to show up or look like a coward to those behind the tasteless act. All the CBS security people were on alert for my arrival, and it gave me some comfort to know that there were many caring employees at the CBS Broadcast Center. It was never discovered who made the call, but I always felt afterward that I was regarded with great respect by the employees at the center.

∽

In my early days at CBS, when I commuted from Queens to Grand Central and walked from the station to the offices on West 52nd Street, my route would take me right past St. Patrick's Cathedral on Fifth Avenue. So I began to stop in briefly

160

and say a quick prayer. I kept it up over the years. Even later in my career, when I had Frank Knapik as a driver, he would drop me off there, and I'd pay a visit, and then walk the block and a half to the office. I knew I had so much to be thankful for.

∽

Negotiating contracts with executives and with on-air talent was a big part of my role as president. In 1980, I had negotiated a new contract with Bob Daly, president of entertainment, and received CBS president Tom Wyman's approval of the deal. But a short time after the agreement was signed, Daly came to me and said he was offered the only job for which he would ever leave CBS. Ted Ashley, the chairman of Warner Brothers Pictures, was retiring and approached Bob to tell him he thought he was the best man to replace him. And he was right!

Bob had started at CBS when he was nineteen years old. He rose through the ranks of business offices, where he negotiated all kinds of contracts with the Hollywood studios and was well respected by that community as a tough but fair negotiator. During his short tenure as president of CBS Entertainment, he led the network back to first place with some solid selections of programming. As much as I did not want him to leave, I knew it was the right thing to do.

Now my challenge was to get Wyman to agree to let Daly out of his contract. Wyman refused to do so. I told him we had no choice. If we forced him to stay, we would have one very unhappy employee. If he succeeded in breaking his contract, we still had to deal with Warner Brothers, one of the major studios supplying network programs. That would not be good for CBS if he left under less than friendly terms. Wyman understood my point and said, "Okay, bitterly, reluctantly." Whatever the reason, I was glad that he agreed to do the right thing.

∽

Ford Motor Company

One day I received a telephone call from the office of Harold "Red" Poling, president of the Ford Motor Company. His representative wanted to arrange a meeting for Poling with me in New York City. This had to be important. Normally, network representatives contacted clients to solicit business or thank them for their business. If the call came the other way, it was usually about some issue of the client's concern.

So I met Poling for lunch in my dining room, and he explained his concerns. The Ford Motor Company was having a difficult year, and Poling was asking all of their suppliers to find ways to lower the cost of their services. He asked if there was any way CBS could lower the cost of our commercial placements. While I was sympathetic to his problem, I said there was no way we could help. Advertising time is a commodity: when demand is high, prices go up. Unlike the Ford Motor Company, which could simply produce more of a popular car to create more inventory, a television network cannot create more inventory. The popularity of a program pushes network prices higher.

While Poling seemed to understand my position, he still invited me to Detroit to hear the presentation they had prepared for their suppliers. I accepted his invitation, and within a week, I flew to Detroit with two of my executives to watch a well-prepared presentation about the problems Ford was facing in the rapidly changing automotive industry. We met in the Ford executive boardroom, which was impressively large. The conference table could seat forty or more people. We sat at one end of the long table, and the presenter stood at a dais at the other end of the room, next to the screen.

From the presentation, I concluded that a Japanese automobile could be sold in downtown Detroit for about $2,500 less than a Ford. Clearly, the Japanese had a competitive advantage that was forcing American automobile manufacturers to take a closer look at their businesses and find reasons why such a pricing differential could exist. Whatever the reason, it had absolutely nothing to do with the price of network television.

Poling understood all of that. He was exploring all avenues of expenditure to see if he could find any efficiencies in the marketing process. He was a particularly good Ford executive. When Ford was having cash and cost problems, he was given responsibility for the North American automobile operations and returned the unit to profitability. He was often given credit for saving Ford in the 1980s.

∾

Ted Turner

One morning in 1985, CBS News president Bill Leonard called me to say he received a phone call from Bob Wussler, a former CBS executive now working as an aide to Ted Turner, the businessman who founded CNN in 1979. He told Leonard that Turner might consider selling CNN, and would CBS be interested in purchasing it? I told Leonard it would be worth discussing the possibility. So we flew to Atlanta for a meeting with Turner and Wussler. They met us at the airport and drove us to a small motel nearby, where they had rented a room for the day.

No sooner did Turner begin the conversation than we realized we were misled. Turner did not want to sell CNN. He wanted to *buy CBS!* As far as I was concerned, the meeting was over. However, Bill and I stayed to listen to Turner talk about how great his company was, how good he was, and how he was going to be wealthier than Bill Paley. While he talked, Turner paced the room, chewing tobacco and frequently spitting the juice into a glass! We sat and listened as he carried on a free-form oration about everything from the state of the business to his personal relations with his wife and family. When he finally finished his rambling, his glass half full of juice, we said we had nothing to discuss. Time to leave.

Leonard and I were angry that we were misled about Turner's plans and flew back to New York. It was just a few months after our meeting in Atlanta that Turner made a concerted effort at a hostile takeover of CBS by using junk bonds, requiring him to break CBS apart to meet the debt requirements. CBS took Turner to court to show why his attempted purchase would be bad for the employees, the corporation, and the shareholders. In a memorandum submitted to the FCC, I argued that CBS would enter into a "death spiral" as a result of the debt required for Turner's takeover. The court sided in favor of CBS, and the Turner attempt to control CBS failed. However, all of the publicity generated by the court case brought CBS to the attention of the Tisch family, and in the end, CBS would not be able to prevent a takeover.

CBS appealed to the Tisch organization, which had holdings in theaters, tobacco and cigarette manufacturing, hotels, and an insurance company, among others, to invest in the company. Because of their assets, the Tisch organization could purchase a large number of CBS shares without incurring any debt. Tisch spent $750 million for a 24.9 percent stake in CBS and a seat on the board. Later, he was named the CEO and company president. So Larry Tisch, a Wall Street trader, did what Turner was unable to do.

When Tisch moved in, Wyman, the president of CBS, moved out. He was rumored to be canoodling with a company employee, showing little respect for Paley, so Paley sided with Tisch and

Wyman was done. With all the turmoil at the corporate level, all I could do was encourage my executives to ignore the disruption and concentrate on doing their jobs. All the corporate activity was beyond our control.

Once the situation calmed down and Tisch was officially the president, Andy Rooney sent me a personal note that simply said, "I'm glad you're still here." As it turned out, Tisch did not have the same standards as Paley and Stanton. He cared little about the image of CBS. All that mattered was money. He slashed jobs, closed news bureaus, ignored management protocol, dictated who should be let go, sold corporate aircraft, making it more difficult for us to visit affiliates, closed group conference rooms, and began selling off important divisions of CBS, including the CBS Music Group, the second largest record company in the world at the time, to Sony. He cut back on building maintenance to the point where Frank Stanton, former president of CBS from 1946 to 1971 and the architect of the CBS "Tiffany" image, said to me, "CBS was just another company, with dirty carpets on the floor."

Westinghouse Electric bought CBS in 1995 for an estimated $5.4 billion, $2 billion of which went to Tisch. Rooney was an outspoken critic of Tisch's, writing in his newspaper column that Tisch's only interest in making a deal to sell CBS to Westinghouse was money. "He turned the best broadcasting company in the business into one of the weakest and got even richer in the process," Rooney wrote. "Large parts of the company were sold off for cash profit that went to Tisch's private company. It's been better for him than it has been for CBS stockholders."

∽

I finally decided that CBS was no longer a company I wanted to work for. It was time for me to leave. So in 1988, I went to Tisch and said I would like to retire at the age of fifty-five years old. I suggested I become non-executive chairman for one year and then leave. He accepted my proposal.

When I told Bill Paley about my plan, he said, "Are you sure you want to do this?" I said yes. The company gave me a dinner in the executive board room, and Paley presented me with the bronze letter "G" from the exterior sign on the original "Columbia Broadcasting System" headquarters building on Madison Avenue.

When I was preparing to leave CBS, I wrote a note to Paley to tell him how much I enjoyed working for him and my career at CBS. I was proud to be associated with such a prestigious and valuable world organization. To my surprise and lasting appreciation, he sent me this personal note:

> Dear Gene:
> Your letter was one of the nicest and most touching letters I have ever received. I cannot answer it in detail, but I can say it was important for me to have you in my life and to be so closely connected in my work. And with this note go my thanks for having done all you did and having contributed so much to making CBS a great network and organization. My very best wishes for the future and more importantly, for a happy and meaningful life.
>
> Sincerely,
> Bill

That note, combined with the farewell dinner for me in the CBS boardroom and Paley's presentation to me of the "G," put a cap on my CBS career. How very fortunate I was.

∾

William Paley died in 1990. He did not live to see the disman-
tling of the outstanding corporation that he built over sixty
years. As a final stamp of dissolution, the iconic CBS headquarters building at 51 West 52nd Street, referred to as "Black Rock"
and home to the corporation since 1965, was sold to outside
investors for $760 million in 2021.

With the loss of the major market leaders, the crown jewel
of CBS programming, *CBS Evening News,* fell into third place,
where it remains to this day. On one occasion I was having
a drink with Mike Wallace and we started to discuss Larry
Tisch. Wallace said, "I hate that man." I said, "Mike, hate is a
terrible word. You can't really mean that." He replied, "I hate
what he has done to the news division with his heavy-handed
decisions."

In 1995, Wallace had been reporting an anti-cigarette story
on *60 Minutes,* and Tisch forbade it from being broadcast, as
part of the Tisch investment portfolio was the Lorillard Tobacco Company. The debacle was made into a movie called *The
Insider*, and eventually the *60 Minutes* story was broadcast.

My last year at CBS was as non-executive chairman of CBS
Broadcasting. I had no decision-making responsibilities, so I
was especially surprised when Neal Pilson, president of CBS
Sports, came into my office all excited to inform me that CBS
had acquired the exclusive rights to Major League Baseball
for $1.8 billion over four years. I was stunned! This was not a
good decision, and based on my experience years earlier with
the league, would only lead to very major and serious financial
losses in the next few years. I was tempted to go to Tisch and
tell him what a terrible decision they'd made. But I did not. The
deal was closed; anything I would say would provoke his anger

and accomplish nothing. He approved the deal; now he had to live with it and suffer the consequences.

And there *were* consequences. CBS wrote off $800 million over the next few years. CBS president Howard Stringer and Neal Pilson both left the company.

The strength of a network is its distribution system, which comprises affiliated stations. Among the more than 200 stations affiliated with CBS were some of the best local television stations in the biggest cities. It is the synergistic effect of a combination of strong local programs and community ties with strong network programs that make the network the best way for advertisers to reach the most television homes in the country. CBS had the best, because they worked hard to maintain strong personal relationships with the owners of the best television organizations. Not only did CBS lose the best stations in major markets, but they went to the fledgling Fox network, strengthening a weak fourth-place operation and causing more financial harm than any other competitor had been able to do in the decades that cable channels had been available.

As mentioned elsewhere, the loss of the strong stations had a devastating impact on the *CBS Evening News*. It only took one meeting for Tisch to damage what had taken years to build. The dynamics of the broadcasting business changed dramatically. Fox became a major player in the network arena and used its success to help build a strong cable identity.

Some years after I retired from CBS, in 1993, I was listening to an early morning CBS news program, and the correspondent said for the first time in decades, CBS would no longer have NFL football games. I let out a screech so loud my wife thought I was having a heart attack. I said that with that loss, things will start falling apart at CBS! Howard Stringer, who followed me as president of the Broadcast Group, openly stated that the NFL now meant No Football Losses for CBS! How wrong he was.

Then came an even bigger business disaster. Ronald O. Perelman, an enterprising financier, acquired a group of television stations from Great American Broadcasters for his company, New World Communications. They included leading stations in major cities such as Dallas, Detroit, Cleveland, and Atlanta, all affiliated with CBS. In 1994, New World management met with CBS executives to seek assurance they would keep the CBS affiliation in future years. CBS made some demands that so offended Perelman's people, they moved all the stations to the Fox network.

This was one of the most momentous decisions in the history of broadcasting. Not only did it strengthen a weak Fox network, it damaged CBS audiences, from which the network suffers to this day. In Detroit, CBS went from a strong Channel 4 VHF station to a much weaker UHF Channel 42. The share of the *60 Minutes* audience in Milwaukee went from thirty-four to seventeen! Furthermore, Channel 42 had no local news to lead into the *CBS Evening News* with Dan Rather. The evening hour with Dan Rather did not lose popularity; the CBS network did!

Similar results were felt in other cities. As a result, the *CBS Evening News* fell into third place, where it still remains more than twenty years later. Fox went on to improve its coverage in twenty-three more markets. As a result, the Fox Network created stronger competition for the three established networks, something cable was not capable of doing for all the years of its existence.

Post CBS

After I retired from CBS in July 1989, Michigan State University invited me to be an adjunct professor in communications. I accepted the offer, and Sally and I moved into an apartment the university provided on the first floor of Shaw Hall, the same dorm I had lived in when I was a graduate student thirty years earlier.

It was a rewarding experience in many ways. Seeing and experiencing the students' curiosity and enthusiasm was stimulating to me. We sat in the president's box for a few football games, rode our bicycles around the campus, had ice cream made fresh in the college creamery, paddled canoes on the Red Cedar River, and played tennis with the varsity tennis coach. When the term ended at the end of the semester, Sally and I were sorry to have to leave. The experience confirmed my belief that Michigan State is a great university with many committed and caring people.

One of the MSU professors, Tom Baldwin, encouraged me to write a book that might have educational benefits for students. When I was finishing my teaching semester, I was asked if I would write an article for the school paper about some aspect or observation of the university during the months I was there. What follows is the text of my article:

Friday, October 20th, began with the glorious aroma of freshly brewed coffee. It was another day of promise! The day itself was cold and damp, and a cup of coffee was the perfect remedy for an otherwise dismal morning. But it was the aroma of the fresh coffee that I remember, a familiar smell that reminded me of other mornings in other places. It is fascinating to me how various scents can resurrect long-forgotten happenings from other times. Events, not important enough to record, brought back by a smell or a fragrance, restored in the forefront of our minds, without any conscious effort to bring them forth—a whiff of lilac reminding one of a first date, the odor of oil for a first car, the smell of leather of a first baseball glove. In the same way that smells can evoke memories, words can too. It was the words spoken by Fred toward the end of the damp, grey day that brought back more memories than that cup of coffee did. Fred was seventy-one years old, twenty of those years as an employee of MSU.

"Remember the iron bridge on Farm Lane?" he said.

"Yes," I said. "It was thirty-one years ago that I saw it for the first time.

"This bridge isn't as nice," he said.

"That's the price of progress," I replied.

"Remember the Quonset huts?" he asked.

"I worked in them for Channel 10," I said. "I was a floor director, assistant floor director, and boom operator on three different shows. I even made a guest appearance to talk about Hawaii on one of the programs."

"They're gone too," he said. "Good riddance. The

new Com Arts building is a vast improvement, in more ways than the obvious ones."

The chance meeting with Fred at the homecoming festivities made me think about a number of other areas that have changed from what I remember thirty years ago. The bare dirt infield housed in the IM building is replaced by tennis courts with a surface that is now artificial. The green grass of the football field in the stadium has been replaced with "turf" that is artificial. The bare dirt floor of Jenison Field House is now replaced with a rubberized surface, obviously artificial. One afternoon I visited the cow barns on College Road to see if some of the cows still had windows in their sides (they do). They are all Guernseys still (because that breed is sturdier; they recover from medical tests while others may succumb). Some of their ancestors used to live across from my dorm, Shaw Hall, in an area now occupied by a multilevel parking garage and Abrams Planetarium. More progress. While reminiscing with one of the managers, he informed me that the bulls that the cows enjoyed occasionally are now in Ohio. Today, even bovine inseminations are artificial!

Fortunately, however, there are some things that are not artificial. They were not thirty years ago, and they are not today. They are, as the saying goes, the real thing! The students and their professors. During these all too short weeks at State, I have had the opportunity to meet, to observe, and to talk with a large number of the college body. I find today's students and teachers to be as attentive, as inquisitive, and as dedicated toward quenching their thirst for knowledge as I believe my generation was thirty years ago. And their task today is much more difficult. Information flows faster, there is more of it, and it changes more rapidly. For the academic body to seek truth requires more effort and more concentration today. I am convinced their generation is up to the task.

This week we leave our home overlooking the Red Cedar to return to our city, that "Baghdad on the Hudson." We will take with us a new set of memories, not of 1959, but of 1989. Years from now, I am sure we will recall events of this time with the same warmth and affection I associate with 1959. Perhaps Thomas Wolfe was wrong! You can go home again! And perhaps Fred is right.

"This is a great school with great people," he said. "I bet our grandchildren will say the same thing."

Even if they never know about the old Farm Lane Bridge.

∽

As a concluding MSU memo stated, "Gene Jankowski will be leaving us on November 3. He has been teaching TC 492/892 as a visiting professor. He also participated in the professional advisory board meetings during October 19 and 20. His insights and optimism have been greatly appreciated and will be missed by his students and colleagues."

∽

Home Sweet Home

Upon returning to Connecticut, I became involved in several pro bono activities. I also served on the boards of the Trans-Lux Corporation, where I was the first non-family chairman of the board, and TV Azteca, a Mexican multimedia conglomerate.

For a few years, I was associated with an investment bank, Veronis, Suhler and Stephenson (now VSS). As a managing director and advisor, I worked with clients in South America, Indonesia, and the Philippines. These engagements enabled me to travel to places like Santiago, Chile (where I went skiing in August), Jakarta, and Manila. Educational in many ways.

Someone once said that "travel is broadening." That is certainly true for my family.

My daughter Jennifer was a junior at Georgetown University, majoring in Chinese in the School of Foreign Service. As a result, she spent a semester in Taiwan at the Mandarin Training Center. When her semester was over, the timing coincided with her sister Judy planning to meet up with her, most likely in Sydney, Australia. That brought forth the idea that their mother should join them for some exciting travel. Sally did not want to go, but I said, if your daughters ask, you must say yes. As a result, Sally met Jennifer in Hong Kong, and the two of them went to Thailand, complete with visits to Bangkok, Phuket, and Chiang Rai. Judy met them in Sydney.

It was December, and we had a tradition of the family always being together at Christmas. So Peter, Carole, and I flew to Sydney and we all had a wonderful holiday week. We went snorkeling at the Great Barrier Reef, boated through to the Daintree Forest, and finished with a visit with Australian media tycoon Kerry Packer at his home. While she was in Sydney, Judy worked for Packer's television network. It was that experience that whetted her desire for a career in journalism.

∾

In 1995, David Fuchs, a colleague and former executive from CBS, and I published a book, *Television, Today and Tomorrow, It Won't Be What You Think,* with Oxford University Press. At the time, the prevailing view was that networks were dinosaurs and would become extinct. We were contrarians, explaining why networks would continue to exist. As of this writing, almost thirty years later, the networks are still here, providing news and entertainment to millions of viewers. The book was even used as a text in communications courses at New York University and Michigan State.

My retirement from CBS coincided with Judy's graduation from college. One of her roommates at school was a student from Kenya, Fiona Pinto, whose parents had a travel service in Nairobi. Judy was spending the summer touring Central Africa with Fiona, who spoke Swahili. During one of her phone calls home, Judy suggested that Sally and I fly to Africa and we all go on a safari. My immediate reaction was: Why would we do that? Once I've seen one elephant, one lion, I've seen them all. But then she said, "Dad, we could climb Mt. Kilimanjaro."

That got my attention.

Kilimanjaro, the highest mountain in Africa and one of the highest peaks in the world. The mountain of legends and folk-lore. The mention of Kilimanjaro got my Ernest Hemingway juices flowing. What a challenge! At fifty-seven years of age, I wondered how my body would react to the altitude of 19,000 feet. Climbers were known to have succumbed to either pulmonary or cerebral edema. Would I be one of them? Nevertheless, I said yes. We would go to Africa, go on a safari, and attempt a climb of Mt. Kilimanjaro.

But we had to try the mountain first. To prepare for the experience, we began a rigorous physical training program during the month of July. I did not want to risk losing any personal physical conditioning by enjoying creature comforts on a six-day safari, complete with food and drinks.

And so we went to Africa. We took six days to climb Mt. Kilimanjaro, and on the ascent passed white crosses where previous climbers had succumbed to one of the edemas (very sobering to see on our way up). Climbers had to be accompanied by sherpas, who carried equipment and food. In our case, we had two sherpas for four people. On the way up the mountain, Judy acquired a stomach bug that sidelined her. Sally, Fiona, and I continued on with the two sherpas, until my wife felt she had to rest, so a sherpa waited with her. Fiona and I continued on with the one remaining sherpa. As we were approaching the summit, Fiona said she could not go on and wanted to turn back. I said she could not do that. If she quit, I would have to go down, too. I was not prepared to quit so close to finishing, after spending days getting to where we were. Stopping was not an option. Fiona was not going to be a quitter, and she wasn't. But as soon as we made the summit, she said goodbye and began her descent. I waited at the top with the sherpa and wondered when the next member of our party would arrive. Soon enough, Sally and her sherpa made it. Mission accomplished! Then the sherpas left us to descend by ourselves. After a few photos of the volcano and each other, we began down the mountain.

After completing the ordeal, Sally and I both agreed that the climb was the most difficult physical thing we had ever done. Once it was over, however, the feeling of exhilaration and glee was unforgettable. Later that year, when I was having my annual physical, my doctor said if he had known what I was going to do, he would have recommended against it! That statement made me feel more elated, as I realized I had tempted fate and won.

∽

After retiring from CBS, I was free to do any number of things, and I did. For one brief moment in 1999, I also started my own company when I acquired the broadcast rights to the Boston Red Sox. They were the main programming of a small New England television network. The following year, I was outbid by the Fox Sports operation. Goodbye, Red Sox. Goodbye, Jankowski Communications System.

∾

By the year 2004, Sally and I were living in Fairfield, Connecticut, and our group of friends began to move south. Some went to Naples, Florida; some to Hilton Head, South Carolina; one to Atlanta; and another to Wilmington, North Carolina. As some of the "older crowd" sold their homes to families with young children, the neighborhood also began to change.

This exodus prompted us to look at our future. But we did not want to move to the south where we did not know people. At that time, we had three married daughters and seven grandchildren in the Alexandria, Virginia, area. While I would not want to move to a child's neighborhood, because that child could be transferred to another part of the country, I felt that the odds of three families moving elsewhere were highly unlikely. So, with little fanfare, Sally and I sold our home in Connecticut and bought a house in Alexandria. In retrospect, it turned out to be the right move at the right time.

∾

Sally's Illness

In 2006, Sally was diagnosed with inoperable lung cancer. She had not smoked since she was twenty-seven years old, so the doctors were quick to conclude that smoking was not the cause. As in many cases like hers, the cause was never known. After a series of radiation treatments, the tumor had shrunk enough that a doctor at Johns Hopkins was willing to undertake an operation. After more than two hours in the operating room, the doctor came out to inform me that he managed to excise all the diseased tissue and what remained was necrotic. We were elated!

After a period of rest and recuperation, Sally and I spent some time at the Greenbrier Hotel, went to Spain where I had been asked to be the keynote speaker at a seminar for Catholic Communications executives, and visited our son Peter and his family in Los Angeles.

Once we were back home, Sally had a memory lapse. An MRI revealed a tumor in her brain. After a year and a half of ups and downs, Sally eventually succumbed to the disease. It was devastating to me and our family. Even before she became ill, she had told me that if anything ever happened to her, I should get married again. She expressed her opinion by stating that life is for the living; one would always have the memories. Furthermore, she said she would consider remarriage a tribute to her time as my wife and mother of our children, whose lives she made meaningful and happy. That she did. She was wonderful in everything she did.

As one of my former neighbors said to me after Sally died, "I don't pray for her, I pray *to* her." What a powerful statement.

∞

Romance Again!

In July of 2007, I was watering some plants in my front yard when a lovely woman and her white Scottie Terrier approached my fence and asked if I was Gene.

"Yes," I said. "Can I help you?"

Her name was Lisa Hayes. She said she had heard I had lost my wife recently and was sorry to hear that. Her husband had died a year earlier, and she could understand what I might be dealing with. That certainly got my attention. In a strange way, just knowing that someone else has suffered a similar painful setback brings a certain emotional comfort. And in an instant, I realized that this woman and I shared feelings that only those who have had similar losses could understand. To put it bluntly, she registered with me! And because of Sally's and my previous conversation about the future, I did not feel guilty about considering another serious relationship.

In the weeks that followed, whether by accident or by design, I began to notice when she was out walking her dog. Hellos became more frequent. I found that besides being beautiful, she was also very intelligent. Over the weeks, then months of that year, our meetings happened more often, our walks more enjoyable, and I began to wonder if there was a possible future for us together.

To learn more about her, I began to introduce her to members of my family, my daughters and grandchildren. On one occasion, my two granddaughters, Julia and Sara, and Lisa and I took a bicycle ride to Mount Vernon, a sixteen-mile round trip, so the girls could form their own opinion about her. Our meetings became so frequent that one of my daughters facetiously asked me if I was getting a dog for Christmas! I then realized that if anything permanent happened with our relationship, my children would not be inheriting a wicked stepmother. And so, after more than a year of a serious courtship, I asked Lisa to marry me. Happily, she said yes.

The following Sunday, when we joined Carole and her family at Sunday mass, Julia looked down the pew at her grandfather with a big smile on her face and gave me a big thumbs up! How great that gesture was!

Lisa and I were married in August 2009 at Holy Trinity Church in Georgetown, in the small chapel dating back to 1789. Reverend William Byron, SJ, pastor of Holy Trinity and an old friend, performed the ceremony. It was the beginning of a new phase in my life filled with home sales and purchases, moving and relocations, meeting and making new friends, and happy days spent with my children and grandchildren. (As of this writing, I await the birth of my first great-grandchild!)

At this point, reflecting on the past, I can think of so many moments when I took risks and enjoyed the rewards, at times even greater than I could ever have anticipated. Lisa and I named our dog, Bailey, after George Bailey, the main character from our favorite movie, *It's a Wonderful Life*.

What a wonderful life, indeed!

Epilogue

Over my twenty-eight years at CBS, I was often described in the press as "optimistic" and "genial." The word "optimism" sometimes troubled me, because when people say, "Oh, he's an optimist," sometimes it has a negative or naïve connotation. Now if it were unfounded optimism, I would agree.

But I think most of my optimism—if that's the word—came from the fact that I had a lot of faith in people. Even from my time in the Navy, or playing baseball, I preferred to start by believing something could get done, because I knew the team was capable of doing it. My optimism was based on a sense of reality and also a wealth of experience.

I also know that if people really believe that they can get something done, they can get it done. Oliver Wendell Holmes said, "If you believe in great things, you may be able to make other people believe in them too." Back in 1971, I went to a class at Harvard University. The professor told us about a case study where they took a man out of the Engineering Department—not an engineer, but a broom-pusher—and gave him different responsibilities and told him that he was capable of them. And the man grew into the position and succeeded beyond his basic abilities, just because he knew people had faith in him, and got the best out of him. I've seen that happen on more than one occasion; I even used that philosophy with my children.

So when I think about whether I am or was an optimist, I would agree that I always started out by thinking that I knew people were capable of doing more than they sometimes thought they could do themselves. (I'd also like to think that I've done my homework first!) If that is how I am remembered, I am at peace with it.

Though life at the highest levels of corporate culture could be stressful and all-encompassing, I always tried to keep my priorities straight. And I had an amazing wife and partner in Sally and now in Lisa. I always said, "Family is first and career is second." If the job didn't work out, I always felt I could get a job someplace else. Of course I aspired to have a good job in broadcasting, and I had one of the best. But we put our family first. I have four terrific kids, one of whom has a major job in the industry, and another who worked in the industry as well.

I have always felt that real happiness doesn't come from money or one's career. If you have good friends and family, you probably can have all the happiness that you want. The fact of the matter is that wealth means nothing if you don't have the relationships and the people.

And the older I get, the more I realize how true that is. I grew up as a very ordinary boy. I believe I had a happy childhood. My father never made it beyond third grade, and my mother never graduated from grammar school because of the conditions at the time. But the fact is that they had a terrific relationship, raised some terrific kids, without the money and everything else that a lot of people have today.

Barbara Bush said it eloquently in her 1990 commencement address at Wellesley College. "Cherish your human connections: your relationships with family and friends. For several years, you've had impressed upon you the importance to your career of dedication and hard work. And, of course, that's true. But as important as your obligations as a doctor, a lawyer, a business leader will be, you are a human being first. And those human connections—with spouses, with children, with friends—are the most important investments you will ever make."

Acknowledgments

There are a lot of people whose presence and influence have had a profound effect on my life. In retrospect, the biggest influence on me was my parents. The standards they set and the loving care they gave me have lasted all my life. Thank you, Mom. Thank you, Dad!

Next, my late wife, Sally, awesome and caring; and my children, Carole, Peter, Judy, and Jennifer. They helped me keep my life in balance. What a team!

My wife, Lisa. Wow! I was fortunate enough to marry a lovely, intelligent, and thoughtful individual. How very, very special she is!

At CBS, Judy Stabile, my secretary and office manager. She was smart, organized, and efficient. Her title then was secretary to the president, but in today's terms, she would aptly hold the title vice president and assistant to the president.

David Fuchs and George Schweitzer were two very important members of my staff. David was great with words, and George was great at public relations. Two solid supporters.

My grammar-school teachers at Public School 69 also had an impact on me. The fact that I still remember their names ratifies that belief. Miss Guinane, Miss Woods, Mrs. Greene, and Miss Flynn were educators who helped me grow intellectually and emotionally. I was very fortunate to have such caring professionals.

More recently, Tom Stanley and Kate Hensler Fogarty. I showed my manuscript to Tom and he said, "Every author needs an editor." He recommended Kate. He was right. As an editor, Kate made my manuscript better!

And special appreciation to the thousands of employees in the CBS Broadcast Group, who allowed CBS to provide the very best information and entertainment programs on the air. Highly talented people.

Perhaps, because of the influence of the Christian Brothers and Jesuit priests, the most important guidepost for me is my religion. Many times I prayed to Jesus for guidance and help. I cannot imagine what my career would have been like without Him!

Appendix A

Interview With The Library Of American Broadcasting, November 7, 1996

In 1995, six years after I retired from CBS, I was asked by the Library of Broadcasting at the University of Maryland if I would consent to an interview to be part of the broadcasting archives. I agreed to the request. What follows in its entirety is the transcript of that interview.

While much of the material was mentioned in the previous chapters, there are additional observations about my experience during my tenure and in the years that followed.

Phil Eberly: This is Thursday morning, November 7, 1996. My name is Phil Eberly, Oral History Project, Library of American Broadcasting. I am fortunate to be with Gene F. Jankowski, whose three decades in the communications industry, twenty-eight of them at CBS, warrants this interview. So thanks again, Gene, for your participation.

Gene Jankowski: My pleasure.

PE: First, let's do a quick biographical sketch of personal aspects of your life outside of the professional zone, which we'll get to momentarily: where you were born, education, and those pertinent things.

GJ: Well, I was born in Buffalo, New York, in my parents' home. I'm a throwback to a different era. I was born in the bedroom, and I had my tonsils out on the kitchen table when I was about six or seven years old. I grew up in Buffalo. I went to college as an undergraduate at Canisius College in Buffalo, a Jesuit school. I, at that time, had to go into the service, so I joined the Navy and received a commission at Newport, Rhode Island's Officer Candidate School. I spent three and a half years in the Navy. I had always wanted to be in journalism. Even as a student in high school, I wrote for the school newspaper and I was editor of the yearbook, and I wrote in college for the school publications. When I was getting out of the Navy, television was starting to grow pretty rapidly and pretty big, and I thought it would be a great opportunity to combine journalism with this new medium of television. So I looked around to see what schools were available that had programs in electronic communications, and at that time Michigan State in East Lansing was one of the major schools that had a good, solid program. There were some technical schools, but I wanted something that also had some liberal arts courses attached to it, so I wound up going to Michigan State where I eventually got my master's degree in radio, television, and film. After that, I went back to Buffalo, got married, wound up working for a small radio station.

PE: Call letters?

GJ: WBNY. It was owned by R. Peter Straus, who at that time also owned WMCA Radio in New York City, and he had thoughts about building a network of radio stations across the state of New York. It didn't work out as well as he had hoped, and eventually he decided he would sell BNY. Since my wife and I were recently married, we said, "Well, here's the best job in broadcasting if we stay in Buffalo, and I think we can do better than that." So we wrote a number of letters to companies we thought we might like to work for in broadcasting, as well as cities where we might like to live. Three of them went to CBS, one to the Radio Network, one to the Personnel Department, and one to Spot Radio Sales. Spot Radio Sales and Network Radio Sales said, "Come on down and we'll interview." The Personnel Department said there were no opportunities at the time, and I learned a great lesson from that. Well, needless to say, I wound up getting an interview with the Radio Network people and I started a week later, September 11, 1961. I spent the next nine years in radio and then went to the television network and did a lot of other fascinating and exciting things during the rest of my twenty-eight years at CBS.

PE: Let's talk a little bit in a more detailed fashion about your radio phase, to begin here. What did you do and so forth?

GJ: Well, as I said, I had my degree in radio, TV, and film, and I had visions of being the world's best producer and director of television programs. When I went back to Buffalo as a young guy out of graduate school, the first thing I ran up against was the thing that most graduate students run up against: no experience. Everybody that wants to hire somebody said, "Where's the experience?" And I used to say, "Well, it's a catch-22. How do I get the job if I don't have the experience, so I can get the experience to get the job?" My first position in Buffalo was working for a small advertising agency, where I would solicit business, write the copy, and then see that the copy was placed on radio stations around the city. In the course of doing that, I received a job offer from one of the radio stations. They asked if I had I ever considered sales? And the frank answer was no, because I used to think sales was selling pots and pans door-to-door to ladies that didn't need them. Eventually, I learned that actually it was probably the most exciting dimension of the broadcasting business, because you had a chance to learn something about a lot of different companies and what their issues were and help solve marketing problems and so forth, and it turned out to be almost more stimulating than what I had originally set out to do. So I took the job at a radio station, feeling that I'd at least get my foot in the door, and who knows what that would lead to. As I mentioned, I was an account executive at WBNY when the station was sold. I wound up getting a job as an account exec at the CBS Radio Network. I was a salesman for five years, and eventually, in my sixth year, I was asked if I'd be the eastern sales manager for the radio network, and I was in that job for almost three years when the television network called to see if I'd consider going to the television network. I felt that every job opportunity really should be looked upon as a chance to learn something. Since I had spent so much time in radio, I thought now getting my foot in the door of television would be a great opportunity to learn something about another dimension of the broadcasting business. I was a network salesman at the CBS Television Network for two years, and I was asked if I would want to be the general sales manager for Channel 2 in New York, that was having a number of troubles at the time. And with the same thought process, I said, "Well, I'll learn something more about local television," since my career up until that point was all network oriented. I took the job and spent about five years in the Television Stations Division as the general sales manager, as the vice president of sales for the division, and as the vice president of finance for about two and a half years. Then I was asked if I would be corporate controller of all CBS at a time when it had seventeen divisions, and I wound up doing that for about a year. The company wound up with a new president who wanted to restructure the corporate staff, and I wound up being put in charge of all CBS corporate personnel, facilities around the world, all the buildings, restaurants, company airplanes, and a school of management that we had started at that time. I was in that position about eight months when I was asked to come back to the Broadcast Group as executive vice president, and then three months later I was made president of all the CBS broadcasting activities. That was in October of 1977.

PE: Okay, thank you. Let's start breaking down into a little bit more detail those eleven years that you were the CEO of all the broadcasting activities at CBS Inc. Let's talk first about the entertainment side of the network. How did you work with those people?

GJ: Well, when we reorganized, we created new divisions. We took the Broadcast Group in October of '77; because it was so large, we actually split it up into a number of divisions and put a president in charge of each one. Bob Daly, who had also had a career at CBS from the time he was nineteen, wound up becoming president of CBS Entertainment in '77. CBS at that time was in third place, and over the next three years we worked to rebuild the schedule, and by 1980, the season of 1980, CBS was again the number one network, with Bob Daly's hard work behind it. I built up some good relationships and some good friendships with the people in the Entertainment Division and in Hollywood. What we did at the time was move the entertainment division to Los Angeles, because up until 1977 Entertainment decisions were primarily made in New York City, and we felt that just as you wouldn't have a sales staff in York, Pennsylvania, if all the activity is on Madison Avenue through advertising agencies, you put your salespeople where the business is. We felt that since so many of the creative ideas were in Hollywood, with all the studios that are out there, we felt that it would make more sense to transfer our Entertainment Division to Los Angeles, and we did that. So we transferred about 200 people out to California so they would have a chance to intermix with the creators of many of the ideas that wound up ultimately on television. It helped the process immediately. So, working with the Entertainment people gave me an opportunity to meet a lot of the studio executives, it gave me a chance to meet a lot of the creators, like Norman Lear, Lee Rich, Zev Braun, etc. A number of times I had dinner with Norman Lear at his home and at restaurants. He was the creator, as we all know, of *All in the Family, One Day at a Time,* and a number of other successful programs. I came to know Lee Rich, who at that time was head of the Lorimar production company that produced *Knots Landing* and Dallas and a number of other big hits. *The Waltons* was their first claim to fame. So it was quite an enjoyable opportunity. I wound up as a young kid wanting to get into broadcasting, and ultimately, I think that as president of CBS Broadcasting, I had the best job in broadcasting that existed in the country. I also liked to play baseball, and as every young fellow who really understands the game, I dreamt of playing center field or pitching for the New York Yankees, and I felt in a sense that's exactly what I was doing when I was running the Broadcasting activities.

PE: Let me ask a question. The stereotype of creative people is that they are somewhat strange, less charitable people than I would say flaky, and how would a, shall we say, person with his feet on the ground, a very oriented person on the bottom line, how did you cope with this sort of free spirit that existed in some of the creative people, both the people that created the product and those that performed in it? How did you manage to cope with this world of show biz that would be counter to your own outlook?

GJ: Well, I think that first of all, too much is made of the so-called flakiness of creative people, because I have always felt that the best people in any walk of life are very creative. I think it's true of your best accountants, I think it's true of your best lawyers, I think it's true of your best engineers, your architects, and it's certainly true of your best business executives: They have an opportunity to see things that other people don't see and they have an ability to make things happen. And I was fortunate enough to have some of the best teachers at CBS, starting with some of the early executives in radio, like George Arkedis and Ben Lockridge, to my almost daily meetings with William Paley at CBS for those eleven years I was president of Broadcasting. It was inevitable that we would interface one-on-one on many, many occasions. Frank Stanton was the president of the company but had retired before I became president of the Broadcast Group, so that gave me a real opportunity to spend more time with Paley than I probably would have had had Frank Stanton still been around. But I think both of those men represent good examples of how you can have strong creative instincts and still be solid businessmen. Much of the CBS image is really the work and the judgment and good taste of Frank Stanton. The sense of style and appearance and look, and the importance of what style can mean to the image of a major corporation, is really what helped make CBS become what we've referred to often as "the Tiffany of the networks." We had programs like *Green Acres,* but it was the overall impact of CBS, the way it was structured, the way we put our programs together, the success of CBS News, the care of the way things looked, whether it was on-air or it was on stationery or in a publication. I think all of that sensitivity is part of the so-called creative process, so I don't think that they're mutually exclusive. As I said, I think some of your best executives in all walks of life have strong creative instincts.

PE: Okay, moving from Entertainment to the News Division. Some of your reflections and perceptions.

GJ: Well, I think that one of the things that we were thankful for in the News Division was that in the period of 1976, shortly before I received the presidency, and through 1980, when CBS had gone from third up to first place, it was the image of the News Division, sort of the jewel in the crown, that kept the affiliates in line. Obviously, when the ratings were down, there was a lot of unrest and uneasiness on the part of affiliated stations because they know that high-rated network programs enhance the image in the local community, and we appreciate that more than anybody else. During that period of time, CBS was the number one news operation, and it was also a period of time when Walter Cronkite was getting ready for his retirement from the anchor chair, so we had a lot of issues to face. Competition from ABC grew stronger, because when CBS had fallen to third place, ABC made a concerted run for stealing some of the CBS affiliates to improve their lineup of stations. And once they started to put ABC on an equal playing field affiliate-wise, it gave them the wherewithal and the financial resources to pay very high salaries for some of CBS's executive news talent. Historians may remember that there was a big attempt at raiding a lot of the stars that CBS had in the News Division, and we had to fight that off. Ultimately, by the 1981 period, after Walter Cronkite had decided it was time to depart that anchor chair, we had decided that the best person to fill that role, because of all the needs that that position requires, was Dan Rather. At that time, Rather was being wooed by ABC. As a matter of fact, I think he was about 90 percent out the door before we made a really concerted effort to persuade him to stay, which he obviously did. I think it's one of the happiest decisions we ever made, because here it is 1996 and he's still, to me, the epitome of what an anchor person should be, in all of the dimensions: not just a person sitting in a chair, but an actual field correspondent who can cover the toughest of stories with the greatest amount of bravery and courage, when necessary under fire, and still represent the network as a first-class individual who can make clients and affiliates and anybody he meets feel very comfortable and at home. The industry itself, not just news but the whole industry, because of what's been happening with the developments in technology, the explosion of cable channels, the development of direct broadcasting, is going through a period of intense competition. The fact that the networks still stand as the epitome of broadcasting—not just CBS, but ABC, NBC—is really a result of the talented people that continue to run the broadcasting operations.

PE: Reports of their demise are vastly [overstated].

GJ: Very much so. Back in 1980, the press was talking about broadcasting stations, and networks particularly, becoming dinosaurs because all these other things were happening out there. People forget that the networks are.

When Stanton retired, Paley had to hire executives to replace him. Eventually, Charles Ireland was hired, who died shortly after from a heart attack. I'm not sure he was the best answer. CBS had a series of executives who had varying strengths, each and every one of them, from Arthur Taylor, who was appointed CBS president at the young age of thirty-seven, to John Backe to Tom Wyman. I can think of positive things to say about each one of them. As a matter of fact, I owe them, each of them, for the success I had at CBS for various reasons.

Arthur Taylor was the one who gave me a chance to get into finance, to be the VP of Finance for the TV Stations Division, which really opened the door for my introduction to the rest of the corporation because of my financial exposure, and I owe him for that. John Backe is the one who asked me to become the president of the Broadcast Group. Tom Wyman was the CEO of the corporation for six years before he left in a lot of turmoil during the hostile junk bond stock market craziness that discombobulated not only CBS, but a lot of other corporations at that point in time. Then came Larry Tisch whom I worked for, for a couple of years, before I decided that I was eligible for retirement and I could still be young enough to do other things. So he and I had a very respectable relationship.

I think he was the wrong man to lead CBS because he didn't understand broadcasting. Basically, he was a Wall Street trader and all he cared about were shareholder values and didn't look upon broadcasting with the same kind of importance and what it really represented as a public trust in the same way that Paley and Stanton did. It was ultimately that thinking that led to the loss of NFL football and the breaking up of CBS as a corporation, with the sale of publishing and Columbia Records and other various and sundry parts.

PE: I don't want to impose on your kindness, but I have some names here in News. Why don't I just go over them, and if you want to stop at any of them, if there's any special reflections. I'll understand you don't want to slight any of them, but I'm mainly concerned about time. Bob Chandler.

GJ: Well, why don't you run down the whole list of them? Because I think that if you begin by saying that anybody is in CBS News, they weren't there by accident; they were there because they had certain skills and talent.

PE: Okay, right. Bob Chandler, Bill Leonard, Bud Benjamin, Van Gordon Sauter, I'll take a deep breath there, Ed Fouhy, Dick Salant, Gordon Manning, Ed Joyce, Bill Small, Bob Wussler, Gene Mater, James Rosenfield, Howard Stringer, Ernie Lieser, Russ Bensly, David Fuchs. A list of colleagues over the years.

GJ: With the one exception, Jimmy Rosenfield was never in the News Division. Jimmy Rosenfield was president of what we called at the Television Network, "sales and affiliate relations." Everybody else in their time at CBS spent their whole career, or a part of it, in the News Division. You just went down, to me, a list of the *Who's Who* of talented people that made CBS News what it was. Some of their careers overlapped, some of their careers were concurrent, and some of them were there when others that you mentioned were not.

I could really do a positive story about every single one of them, and we could be here for another four hours, but two people that I would mention of the list, just to single them out, would be first Bill Leonard. Bill Leonard was a terrific producer who was one of the creators or co-creators of *60 Minutes*. What's the saying? "Success has many fathers, failure is an orphan"? The success of *60 Minutes* has led to a lot of people taking credit for the creation of the program, and I really think it is more a collaborative effort between Don Hewitt and Bill Leonard. Bill Leonard was in charge of news specials at a time when Don Hewitt was a producer of the hard news programs who said there should be a place for programs, stories that don't fit into the evening news. But Bill Leonard was there at the beginning. Bill had left CBS News and was running the CBS office in Washington, D.C., not for News but for the corporation. He was the liaison between CBS management and the FCC, senators and congressmen who wanted to talk to CBS or had an issue, corporate liaison in all broadcasting matters, if you will. When we knew that Dick Salant was going to retire, we needed a replacement as the president of CBS News. I persuaded John Backe that the guy that should get the job is Bill Leonard, even though he had a year or so before retirement. I felt Paley would probably make an exception since he knew him well, and he was the best man around to take CBS News through a transition period until we appointed a successor. Bill did that job for two years, and it was on his watch that he and I worked very, very hard to hold on to Dan Rather. I can't say enough nice things about Bill Leonard and his abilities as an executive, as a creator, and as an innovator, and as just an all-around good person.

Van Sauter, I think, is one of the most misunderstood and misrepresented people, because he got caught in the industry at a time when there were corporate changeovers. But to Van I give credit for salvaging the first year's performance of the *Evening News* under Dan Rather. Sauter again has a very strong feeling of what looks good on the screen, and while he has other habits, if you will, that trouble some people from time to time—somebody had described him as having sand in his shoes—but he was to me one of the best troubleshooters. You could take Sauter and give him a problem and he would resolve it. It was true when you needed somebody to run a television station and turn it around, which he did in Chicago and Los Angeles, to having someone take the Sports Division and turn that around, which he did, to salvaging the News Division during a period of turmoil, which he did, and helped Dan Rather's *Evening News* broadcast become the number one evening news broadcast back in the early ' 80s.

The other names you've got, as I said, we could go on for a number of hours here, but just a litany of a lot of talented people who kept the broadcast operations going under extremely difficult times. Let me add to that list just a fast rundown: Charles Kuralt, Bill Moyers, Mike Wallace, Sandy Socolow, Walter Cronkite, Don Hewitt, Andy Lack, and John Lane. Different connections with the news from one point or another.

Oh yes, every one of them. That is a Who's Who of the journalistic fraternity, and every one of them is a topnotch individual. I was sorry to see Moyers go back to public broadcasting, but he is an extremely talented guy.

Charles Kuralt to me was one of the brains of CBS News because he was so unique in his style and his original concept about touching American people—unsurpassable. Interesting enough, last month Charles was honored by the Academy of Television Arts and Sciences, and among five other Hollywood types, from Hollywood producers to personalities from television shows, Kuralt was the only newsman. Of the six, Charles was the only man that didn't have a prepared script, he was the only one that didn't have film clips, he was the only one that didn't have three other people speak on his behalf before he got up with his acceptance speech, and yet, the minute Kuralt was introduced, he had a standing ovation. He spoke off-the-cuff for about three minutes, finished, and received another standing ovation. He touched everybody in the room. It sort of reminded me of [what] it must have been like with Lincoln and his Gettysburg address. It was a short speech, but he captured the audience. He's terrific. If you could have five more Charles Kuralts in all the different places, you wouldn't have to worry about the competition.

PE: In a highly regulated industry such as broadcasting, you alluded to the FCC and a Washington presence. Did that take a lot of your time?

GJ: Yes. Two things that were more prevalent back then that I don't see or read as much about now: There were pressure groups, from the Reverend Donald Wildmon to Reed Irvine and AIM, who appeared back then to be more vocal than they are now. There were more hearings, it seems to me, from the Fritz Hollings Senate subcommittees to Ed Markey to Jim Wright, all wanting to ask a lot of questions.

As a matter of fact, out of all that, I maintained that, with all the new channels, the biggest problem that the broadcasting industry had to worry about was the content of programs coming over the tube provided by pay television and cable channels. The fact is they all came out of the same box in the living room. We were all in the same boat, and their end was sinking. The fact of the matter was that my thoughts and my premise were sustained not too long after I expressed them to some of my colleagues. Senator Lautenberg from New Jersey saw a very strong R-rated movie on his cable channel. He was so incensed he demanded hearings and wanted all the networks to provide educational programming as a result of what pay television was doing. So the broadcasters were getting blamed for the content provided over the same screen by other sources. We would always argue that our standards were above reproach, that we didn't have frontal nudity or any kind of nudity on television, that we did have standards and practices, we stood for something, and unfortunately a lot of the other program suppliers did not. I'm happy to see that one of the programs that CBS was carrying, *Public Morals,* this year was canceled very quickly because I'm told it had language that most of us wouldn't want to have spoken, we don't use, and wouldn't want to have spoken to us in front of our family. I'm happy the public was judgmental enough not to watch that kind of stuff.

I do worry that some producers, in trying to push the envelope, keep trying to get their standards of taste and morals to be the public's standards, and I think it's a tragic mistake when broadcasters don't stand up for what they are responsible for. I really do believe that ultimately the responsibility rests with the individual station operator, individual management, in terms of whether or not certain kinds of programming or program content goes out over their airwaves. The minute we start to lose our standards, I think we sow the seeds for future problems for the industry. Television has always been an invited guest in people's homes. To assure financial success you have to make sure you're invited back every day, day after day, week after week.

The minute we do things to make us an uninvited guest, we start to sow the seeds for our own demise as an industry, and I would hate to see that happen.

PE: There's a lot of talk today, both on the political front and the general news front, about the cultural rot and so forth. Now that you're back, take a different look at it, does this trouble you that TV is contributing perhaps to this so-called cultural rot that some people talk about?

GJ: We're all responsible for our own individual behavior; and when we have young children, we're responsible for the way they're brought up. I don't think television causes things to happen any more than reading a book causes something to happen. It may affect our thinking on certain topics, but ultimately each of us as an individual is sort of a tapestry that's made up of a lot of forces experienced over our lifetimes, from the parents we had, to the schools we went to, the friends we hung around with, the things we watched perhaps, the things we read, and ultimately we filter it all and take actions as an individual that are either good or they're bad, or some combination thereof. I don't think it's fair to blame the TV medium for the problems in society.

I'd say one of the best research projects existed in Russia where the government controlled all the means of communication. The government controlled what people saw and heard and read, and yet the more the government turned on the messages, the more the people turned them off, and ultimately the Iron Curtain came down because people didn't like what they were hearing. That's an oversimplification, but what I'm really pointing out is that just because the messages can be controlled doesn't mean the people are going to be controlled. I don't think people are robotic individuals or sponges that absorb everything they see on television. Indeed, if that were the case, there probably wouldn't be any criticism about what they watch. But people do make a valid judgment when they turn a program on, and their judgment either says, "I will sit and watch this," or "I can't stand it"; and if it's bad enough, they not only maybe can't stand it, they'll complain about it. And I think that that's all for the good. But to blame the medium is to look for false answers to more serious issues. It doesn't mean that we shouldn't be responsible for what we put on, because I do think that broadcasting has ratifying elements to it, that if we behave one way and then we see somebody on television behaving the same way, it sort of ratifies what we're doing. If we behave one way and we see television doing something different, it doesn't mean we're going to change, but it might make us think about what we're doing.

PE: Anything you might want to say about those bizarre attempts to takeover? You alluded to one, the Ted Turner thing, and then the other one, the Jesse Helms thing. Did that take a lot of your time?

GJ: Yes. The first attempt really was because of the craze of junk bonds. Ted Turner made an approach to buy CBS, and in so doing he would have incurred so much debt that CBS would have had to sell off its major pieces just to cover the debt, and I think it would have meant the demise of CBS. It would have pulled apart CBS as CBS should have been. And we fought that off very successfully. Some people tried to say that when Larry Tisch took over the company that, in effect, he did exactly what Turner was going to do, and I say that is not true. Tisch did not inherit a lot of debt. CBS didn't have much debt. Tisch sold off the different divisions, like Records, not to cover the debt, but to generate cash, which ultimately was parceled out to shareholders. So it was completely different. In one case, the shareholders benefited financially, short-term, and in the other case they wouldn't have benefited at all. But even in the Tisch takeover situation—it wasn't a takeover technically, but in his management of the company—I maintain that because of the loss of football, because of the loss of the stronger affiliates, on a long-term basis, the shareholders were shortchanged. There were shareholders who picked up some fast money and ran, but for those people that were looking for an annuity that would have gone on for a long period of time with a healthier company in a healthier industry, I think that on a long-term basis there are a lot of losses.

Jesse Helms? Jesse Helms has wanted to talk about being Dan Rather's boss kind of a thing. I put Jesse Helms in the same category of the Reed Irvines of the world and the Frank Lautenbergs: they're well-intentioned people, but they have a misunderstanding of how the process works. I believe ultimately, if you really think about it, it shows a lack of respect for the viewing audience. But at the same time, I've been around long enough to realize what is purely political and intended to make political gain. In Jesse Helms' case, I guess it works on his behalf because he was just reelected this past Tuesday (chuckling).

PE: Quickly, your continued links to academia. Now in this phase of your career, what are you doing in that regard?

GJ: Well, I've been an adjunct professor at Michigan State University. When I retired from CBS, that first fall semester my wife and I went to East Lansing and I taught a graduate course, a full-credit course to graduate students in radio, television, and communications. I've been on the board of three universities counting Canisius College, Georgetown University, and Catholic University. My terms are finished. I've written a book, published last year by Oxford University Press.

PE: Thank you for sending me a copy. I wanted to get to that next.

GJ: Okay. That publication really came out of the fall semester that I spent at East Lansing when the professors encouraged me to write a book on the industry as I saw it, because they don't really have a book written by anybody who lived the business and been in a position—

PE: Well, you could publish and not perish at the same time.

GJ: That's right, I could (chuckling). It was an enjoyable experience. It gave me a chance to share a lot of philosophies that I have about the industry and where it's going and what it is and what it isn't. But in other academic things, I maintain a liaison with some university presidents. John De Biaggio, who used to be president of Michigan State, is now president of Tufts University in Boston, is a friend of mine, and when we get together, we talk about the industry and academia. I have had discussions with one major university that has a commercial television station to see what we can do together. I'm in the midst of discussions with them right now, as a matter of fact, how we can program a television station to serve the community. That's a commercial station not affiliated with a television network. So, through various and sundry forms, I keep involved.

PE: You're too modest about your activities in the public square. That's on the record in your biographical material, so I'll let that go. In wrapping it up, I think we mentioned the name before in setting up this appointment, Larry Grogan, who was a classmate of yours or you knew him in Buffalo?

GJ: Larry Grogan. I knew him in Buffalo when I was starting

out in the industry as a young salesman. Larry Grogan, if memory serves me, was a salesman for WBEN, a radio station in Buffalo. At that time, Mrs. Butler owned the *Buffalo Evening News* newspaper, she owned an AM, an FM, and a television station, and every single one of them was the best, they were number one. As a matter of fact, I interviewed with WBEN Television. The general manager of that station was a man named George Torge, and when I said earlier I looked at what would be the best job in Buffalo if I stayed in Buffalo, it was that job, working for the best television station in the city. And I said we could do better than that if we got out of town (chuckling). But Larry Grogan was part of that process and part of that company back then.

PE: I ran into Larry last week. He's with Susquehanna, and I said, "I'm going to have the privilege of getting you into one of these oral histories." And I said, "If I had to in a business way characterize your career, the first expression that would come to the top of the list would be consensus builder." I said to Larry, "That's what impresses me." And without missing a beat, Larry said, "Well, that was his good training with the Jesuits along the way." I've always had a lot of respect for the Jesuits as scholarly types.

GJ: So do I.

PE: That certainly rubbed off, no question about it.

GJ: Oh, I still maintain my close contacts. Vincent Cook is president of Canisius College now, and he and I have talked recently. But there's a lot to that. I think that the Jesuit training held me in good stead.

PE: After twenty-eight years in the corporate culture, basically at CBS, to be able to handle that with a very successful personal life and everything, it is a strength that I think people that will go to this tape should be aware of. I don't know why, but broadcasting—maybe it's because I was in it—has always had a record or a reputation for being particularly venomous in the political sphere of business, which is not true, as I know, but it has that reputation. But here you are, twenty-eight years in the same vineyard. I just think it's remarkable, and I compliment you.

GJ: (chuckling) Well, it's interesting to hear it expressed in those terms. I have never looked at it that way. What I've always tried to do, and fortunately I've got a terrific wife, but we've always kept our priorities straight. I have always said "family is first and the career is second." And if the job doesn't work out, we [can] always go get a job someplace else. I aspired to have a good job in broadcasting; as I mentioned, I had one of the best, but we put our family first. We have four terrific kids, one of whom has a major job in the industry, and one who has a very good job in the industry—on their volition, not because of anything I did—and it's working out very well for them. But we always said that if the job doesn't work, we'll go do something else.

But it's sad, the tragedy that I see and have seen, not only in this industry, but other industries, is when people put the job first to the exclusion of the family or to the breakup of the family. I have always felt that real happiness doesn't come from the amount of money or the job, it really comes from the people that you know. If you have good friends and good family, you probably can have all the happiness that you want. The other things can make it easier, but the fact of the matter is your wealth means nothing if you don't have the relationships and the people and the knowledge.

I think Barbara Bush said it very eloquently when she made a commencement address. An all-women's college wanted her to speak, and it got to be very controversial at the time as they thought she was the wrong person to come out and speak. She showed up, and the thing that I remember about her comments was just that. She said, "Look at all this other stuff that people get excited about. It will be forgotten, and it doesn't mean anything. The only thing that really matters is family and friends."

And the older I get, the more I realize how true that is. I grew up as a very ordinary boy. I believe I had a happy childhood. My father never got beyond third grade, and my mother never graduated from grammar school because of the conditions at the time. But the fact is that they had a terrific relationship, raised some terrific kids, without the dollars and everything else that a lot of people have today.

PE: Well, thank you very much, Gene. First of all, I'll repeat the transcript editing if you wish. Secondly, if you have any memorabilia, any artifacts, when you clean your closet out sometime, before you put out the yard sale sign, maybe think about the Library of American Broadcasting, if you will.

GJ: I will. I have the flyer that was sent.

PE: I appreciate it very much, and I'll see that this is sent to the proper place. And once again, thank you so much.

GJ: Thank you.

Appendix B

Awards and Tributes

- Gene F. Jankowski Scholarship in Telecommunication at Michigan State University: The scholarship is awarded to African American students or graduates of Detroit public high schools with an excellent academic record and demonstrated leadership ability through extracurricular involvement.
- Gene F. Jankowski Award of Excellence at Canisius University: The award is given to a graduating senior in Communication Studies or Digital Media Arts who has demonstrated academic excellence.
- National Education Association Advancement of Learning through Television
- International Radio and Television Faculty Industry Service, 1973
- Outstanding Alumni Award, Michigan State University College of Communication Arts/Science, 1990
- Good Scout Award—BSA, 1983

- American Red Cross Certificate of Appreciation, Board of Governors, 1984–1992
- Adjunct Professor of Communications, Michigan State University
- Director, St. Vincent's Hospital, Bridgeport, Connecticut
- Chairman of the Board, St. Vincent's Hospital School of Nursing
- Director of Board, Georgetown University
- Board of Directors, Catholic University
- Board of Directors, Canisius College
- American Film Institute
  - Member, Board of Trustees
  - Member of Executive Committee
  - Chairman of Board
- Honorary Doctor Degrees: Michigan State University, Canisius College
- Board of Directors, Television Azteca, Mexico
- Distinguished Alumni Awards: Michigan State University, Canisius College
- Trans-Lux Corporation
  - Board Member
  - Chairman of Board
- Director, CASA—Center for Alcohol and Substance Abuse
- Knight of Malta
- International Academy of Television Arts and Sciences
  - Board Member
  - President
  - Fellow
- Board Member, American Advertising Federation
- Executive in Residence, St. Bonaventure University, 1983
- American Women in Radio and Television, 1984

- Media Award, Polish American Congress, 1979
- Distinguished Communication Medal, Southern Baptists
- Polish World American Citizen of the Year, 1979
- Giant of Broadcasting
- Buffalo Broadcaster Hall of Fame, 2022
- *Variety* Children Charity Heart to Heart Humanitarian Award, 1986
- National Conference of Christians and Jews Humanitarian Award
- Avatar Award Broadcast Financial Management

www.ingramcontent.com/pod-product-compliance
Lightning Source LLC
Chambersburg PA
CBHW031503120626
46545CB00005B/1726